MW01041332

Secrets Of The List

The Key To Direct Marketing Using Email and Social Media

by David M. Ross

Copyright © 2012 by David M. Ross
All rights reserved.

Published by BossRoss Media, Nashville, Tennessee

No part of this book may be used or reproduced in any form or by any means, electronic or mechanical without written permission from the publisher.

For more information contact BossRoss Media,
1231 17th Ave. S. Nashville, TN 37212

ISBN: 1475009321
ISBN-13: 978-1475009323

Back Cover Photo: Isabel W. Ross
www.izzynashville.com

Secrets Of The List is dedicated to:
Marion and Martin Ross whose love and support has guided me for a lifetime. From my earliest years they believed in me and taught me to believe in myself.

Connecting...

http://www.SecretsoftheList.com

Twitter: @davidmross

Facebook:
www.facebook.com/davidmross
www.facebook.com/secretsofthelist

Table Of Contents Chapters

Appendices

ACKNOWLEDGEMENTS

Secrets Of The List has been a labor of love thanks to my enormous support team. Although I have been writing professionally as a journalist for over 30 years, this is my first book and I wasn't sure what it would be like. It turned out to be an enjoyable experience.

There's lots of folks to thank for helping me achieve this milestone. First I'd like to thank Edward Morris and Robert K. Oermann whose unique writing styles taught me many years ago about the importance of colorful phrasing, having something to say *before* you write and being concise. I'd also like to thank the Nashville music community for supporting *MusicRow* magazine since its first issue in 1981. That became the platform that allowed me to develop my skills as a writer.

Team members are so crucial to a project's success and I've been fortunate to assemble some great professionals. Cronin Creative's Karen and Peter Cronin were responsible for the unique book cover design. I envisioned something strong and recognizable and they delivered. Thanks guys! Also Sarah Skates took on the task of proofreading the final manuscript. Her diligence resulted in many improvements for which I'll be forever grateful. Author/technologist Jay Frank was also extremely helpful in guiding me through the publishing maze. His recent books served as an inspiration. Industry friend Woody Bomar provided several key ideas and special thanks to Jeff

Walker and AristoMedia for public relations support. I'd also like to thank Jaron Lowenstein, Tony Conway, Larry Pareigis, Kevin Mason and Jennie Smythe for their invaluable insights.

As for my personal support team, I wonder sometimes if they secretly got together and strategized how to keep me motivated and productive. Included on the cheerleading squad are my two daughters Michelle and Isabel, my son in law Tim Stephens and Isabel's friend Daniel Martin. And of course my wife Susana, who after 36 years of marriage reads *me* like a book and always seems to know when I need a little push.

Last, but not least I'd like to acknowledge the late Steve Jobs. I never met the man, but his visions changed my life. My first Apple Plus computer in the early eighties led to desktop publishing and databases and opened my career from a pathway to a highway. Up until his untimely death, Jobs continued to redefine the worlds of music and media with impactful new technology. Thank you Mr. Jobs.

—David M. Ross, March 11, 2012

Chapter 1
The Secrets
Are Solid

What if you could grow your company's bottom line, become more competitive, acquire new customers and enhance your ability to market more effectively without breaking the bank? Would you take some time to read how? Of course you would.

Secrets Of The List is dedicated to helping you do just that—make more money and take advantage of digital marketing opportunities using email and social media. As an added bonus, you will also create a consumer army of dedicated brand supporters invaluable for feedback as your company grows and considers new offerings. Right now you're thinking, "But we don't have thousands of dollars to allocate for marketing." Forget that. These concepts can be implemented with little or no added expense, using tools you likely already have, like a computer and an Internet connection. That's the purpose of this book, to pull back the curtain on some of the most powerful ideas in marketing today and show you how to begin profiting by harnessing their power. Welcome to the *Secrets of The List*.

The "secrets" are solid. They are tried and true direct marketing ideas that have been working for many decades in analog form. But traditionally, this valuable tool has remained out of reach for many small and medium size companies because of the high costs of creating, printing, targeting and mailing materials. Happily, those expensive parts can be reshaped to fit into today's digital information engines. In fact, thanks to the one-to-one essence of the Internet, the direct marketing ideas detailed in this book are more cost effective, AND MORE VALUABLE than ever before.

As this book is being written (Nov. 2011) unemployment remains above 9% where it has been since 2009[1]. It's likely we are seeing a major societal shift in addition to economic turmoil. In the early 1900s the transition from agrarian to industrial economy created severe disruption in the labor force. Today, we are again experiencing sweeping change as we further evolve from an industrial economy into a data-driven information age. But along with hardships for some, this digital frontier presents incredible opportunities.

For most people suffering unemployment there comes a time when waiting around for the "perfect job" is simply no longer an option. They need to make a living and they need to do it—NOW! More and more brave-by-necessity entrepreneurs are being forced to start their own companies. As a person who successfully started a company and sold it 30 years later in a multi-million dollar deal, I can tell you running a successful company is not just about being

---

1 http://www.bls.gov/cps/tables.htm#empstat

frugal. Customer acquisition is equally essential. And that is another way of looking at the purpose behind using the *Secrets of the List*—to build a loyal customer base. If you have a small or medium size company which you would like to market more effectively so it can grow and become more competitive, this book is especially for you. Hopefully, by now I've got your attention, so let's dig in and get started. But first I'd like to say, "Thanks for joining me, on this digital journey." If you have any questions or comments along the way, contact me directly at dross@bossross.com.

The Appendices

When thinking about digital marketing it's helpful to move once in a while from the micro to the macro view. Consequently, there are four additional "macro" articles at the end of this book, each of which is included for different reasons. As you travel through the main chapters of this book I encourage you to veer off and thumb through each of the appendices as desired. They do not have to be read in any particular sequence.

Chapter 2
Lemonade Stand Lessons And The Power Of Email

The concept of being able to speak directly with your customer or potential customer is easy to grasp. It feels intuitive. Many of us learned variations of this lesson as little kids with our first lemonade stand. Nothing happened until someone arrived, either by car or on foot. We hoped they would buy some of the freshly made drink. Unfortunately, only a few passers by actually took the time to stop and boost a kid's self-esteem. As a result, some kids learned that having your own business is disappointing and can lead to failure. While others (more confident) realized that having your own business presents a problem which must be solved—getting more customers to come by your stand. The really smart kids also realized that their odds of making a sale would be even higher if they could move the stand someplace near lots of thirsty customers.

• • •

In its most basic form, the "list" is a collection of email addresses and perhaps other data such as gender, zip code or year of birth. Since this book is about the creation and strategic use of such a list, plus engaging and aggregating an online social networking audience, let's discuss exactly why these tools are so valuable.

Music City Networks is a Nashville-based web development and interactive media company, founded in 2001 whose clients include many of Nashville's top stars. The company released a study titled *The True Value of an Email Address*. This writer covered their research for industry trade publication *MusicRow* in an exclusive interview on Sept. 9, 2009. The findings were eye-opening. Here's a few key excerpts from that article.[2]

"Artists and record labels historically had little or no direct fan relationships. CDs were shipped, placed on store shelves and the identities of purchasers were mostly a mystery. As a result, marketers had to use shotguns instead of sniper rifles when creating advertising campaigns. The Internet, email and social networks have rapidly changed that equation as shown by a new study completed by Music City Networks, 'The True Value of an Email Address.' The study compiles responses from 1384 random fans who opted into the databases of eight artists inside the MCN network. It studies behavior over a two year period.

---

2 Study Proves Email Value, writer: David M. Ross ©2009 MusicRow Enterprises. Used by permission.

Top level findings showed that the average fan email address is worth $111 per year in artist revenue both online and off. 'Of that $111,' said MCN President Lang Scott, 'the vast majority is being spent away from their website ($98) on artist stimulated revenue streams like iTunes, Ticketmaster, and at retail stores.' According to the study, only about 38% of users actually make purchases, therefore the key ingredient in increasing revenue is building the number of unique visitors to the website and the size of the total email network."

The study proved that engaging customers online would yield future purchases.

"It reinforces the fact that artists should be making every effort to acquire email addresses," Tim Putnam, MCN Partner and VP of Marketing told *MusicRow*. MCN Partner Paul McCulloch summed it nicely, "Developing a fan database is career critical."

The web is alive with articles about the power of email marketing. G. Simms Jenkins notes, "Email marketing is simply the best way to communicate with customers and those who could become customers. New research shows that 50% of surveyed consumers are more likely to buy products from companies that send them email, whether their purchases are online or at a place of business."

Jenkins advises companies to be consistent with respect to messaging through email. "Bad email can be damaging well beyond the inbox," he warns. "Give consumers exclusive content, offers, and reasons to become and stay a subscriber. Sometimes the best thing you can do is say 'thanks' to your customers."

The above 2009 excerpts show the power of the email database has been widely recognized for years. But something monumental has changed since 2009—social media. Simply stated that means Facebook, (currently with over 850 million users worldwide), Twitter, YouTube and MySpace—the big dogs on the field—plus a variety of smaller, but substantial social networks such as GetGlue, Google+, Foursquare, Linkedin, Pinterest and more.

The rise of social networks has altered forever the marketing landscape for small and medium size brands. Previously, purchasing a marketing database meant investing in a large hit or miss experiment combined with the slow process of reaching out to people individually at company events and other in-person opportunities. Social networking has changed that and become a massive gift for marketers.

An Oct. 12, 2011 MediaPost[3] article by Cory Treffiletti, sums the marketing and revenue value of social networking by effectively saying companies will get out of it what they put into it.

"The future of online media is most definitely rooted in brand marketing. Brands are seeing that it's important to

---

3 The Future Of Social Media: Is It Branding?, Cory Treffiletti. Mediapost, 2011.
http://www.mediapost.com/publications/article/160353/the-future-of-social-media-is-it-branding.html

build frequency in the eyes of the target audience, and eliminate wasted impressions against those people you are not interested in speaking to. If the brand utilizes its social platform in an economical, engagement-driven manner, then the value [of a fan or follower] can be high."

And that's what the *Secrets of the List* is all about, connecting with the people most likely to be interested in your product or service. It's impressive to have large lists, but not everyone represents the same revenue-stream value to your company. Some of those interested fans are really "thirsty" for what you offer, while others are content to sit back and casually observe. It's about level of engagement. After all it doesn't take much dedication to follow a brand on Twitter. Whereas spending dollars on a company's goods or services is a much more engaged behavior.

So *Secrets of The List* isn't just about numbers or names. It's about connecting with specially qualified names—super fans that are thirsty for what you have to offer and want to spend money to get it. But don't be too hasty about excluding folks who have expressed a more casual interest. It's possible some of them might become more interested. They might even become super fans, someday. And just as importantly, they might also help you attract additional super fans through word of mouth (WOM). WOM is not a new concept, but it has been supercharged by social networking. Let's take a closer look at how levels of engagement translate into behavior. Every consumer/ fan may not fit the table below precisely, but it's a good overview of how the process works. Engagement can be segmented into four levels; Low, Medium, High and Heavy.

The Engagement/Behavior Matrix

The process begins once a consumer clicks on your Facebook page, follows you on Twitter, or enters into a relationship on another social network like YouTube or Google+. Once they connect with the brand in this way, it becomes more likely they will occasionally click on a link from the brand that is part of a post or Tweet. These activities are consistent with a Low level of Engagement. The consumer decides how often they want to interact with the brand, and the brand must try to increase that frequency by offering information, content, special offers, coupons, etc. that attract the consumer's interest and motivate them. When a consumer signs up to follow or like a

Brand Engagement Behavior (Part A)

Engagement Level	Likes/ Follows Brand	Sometimes Clicks On Brand Links	Regularly Visits Brand Website (Via Links Or Directly)
Low	√	√	
Medium	√	√	√
High	√	√	√
Heavy	√	√	√

brand, they aren't promising anything. No minimum number of clicks, or special attention of any kind. If the brand wants more clicks it has to earn that behavior by sending out content that consumers value.

A frequent question is, "Which social networks should my brand be on?" The answer is, "All of them." Facebook is by far the largest of all the social networks, but some consumers don't like Facebook, they are more comfortable on YouTube and/or Twitter. Since our goal must always be to reach the largest total number of fans and potential fans, a brand should be ubiquitous across all networks. In the digital world, there is no one big thing.

There are lots of choices. As a result, a brand must try to insert itself everywhere that possible fans might be. (Situations where an unwary consumer gets added to a list without realizing it—maybe at a cash register or when

Brand Engagement Behavior (Part B)

Engagement Level	Subscribe To Brand Email List	Regular Messages Place Brand Top Of Mind	Become WOM Brand Evangelist
Low			
Medium			
High	√	√	
Heavy	√	√	√

purchasing online can be assumed to be Low Engagement even though you already have the consumer's email.)

Low Engagement

Social network contact is unpredictable. Will the consumer find your message in a vast stream of Tweets? Sometimes. Facebook's posts are even more complex. It uses an algorithm called Edge Rank, to decide how important your post is to each individual connected to you. If the algorithm doesn't think the user finds your info useful, based upon past behavior, then they may not even see it. That's right, whether you have 100 or one million Likes, doesn't mean that every one of those individuals will actually see what you are sending out. This uncertainty makes it even more important to be visible on as many networks as possible.

Medium Engagement

Once a consumer starts to enjoy the relationship with a brand, i.e. finds value, they might start to visit the brand's web page directly in addition to clicking on links in posts that are offered in the various social network streams. This behavior places them in the Medium engagement category because the brand is becoming a bit more top of mind. Medium engagement might also mean that a consumer makes sure to connect with the brand on multiple social networks. Moving from Low to Medium is perhaps the most important step in the engagement/behavior matrix.

Why? Because the consumer is identifying themself as a prospect for even higher levels of engagement. Once this higher level of engagement begins, there is a good chance it will eventually lead to revenue. Perhaps the revenue will be related to something online, or as noted in the Music City Networks research at the beginning of this chapter, it may be generated in the physical world. Either way, this is great news for the brand.

High Engagement

Moving from Medium to High engagement is signaled when the fan takes the welcome step of offering his or her email address to the brand. This is an amazing moment in the brand/user relationship and should not be taken lightly. Welcome the new consumer and make them feel appreciated. Now the brand has the unprecedented ability to contact the consumer on *its* schedule. The opportunities which this presents are powerful and revenue producing.

Heavy Engagement

Somewhere in this process the High engagement person graduates to Heavy engagement as their interaction expands and they become word-of-mouth (WOM) evangelists helping to spread the message through clicks and by talking about it to their friends. After hard work, attention to detail and consistency, we finally have a person who is receiving our regularly scheduled email messages, plus staying in touch via the social networks. They are likely visiting the brand's site a few times or more each week and engaging with the content. Perhaps they are commenting on a few articles or downloading a coupon. Hopefully, they are also clicking on the viral social network sharing buttons found at the bottom of each article which further spreads the brand's story. Heavy Engagement and sharing is of high value to the brand, introducing it to new consumers and widening its circle of influence.

The Carrot or the Stick?...

With regard to technology, it is all about the carrot. You have to motivate people to come to you. You do that by enticing them with things that are unique. Yes, it may be possible from time to time to use the stick in very sophisticated ways to punish inaction, but until a person has opted in to become part of your brand's world by giving permission to contact them (via email), there are only limited options available to contact them, regardless how sophisticated the approach.

Happily, there are many creative ways to stimulate the engagement process. You are likely blessed with valuable additional assets. Start thinking about how to leverage them. Maybe it's creating content that explains new ways to better use the product. Does your brand have a celebrity spokesperson that might participate from time to time in some way? And what about the consumers themselves? Give them a chance to be part of the page and they will surprise you with what they are willing to contribute. What works best for you might be a contest where fans upload photos or stories of how they use the brand, or why. This is an area where creativity and experimentation can be a powerful force to grow your brand and attract and mobilize engagement.

Country superstars Lady Antebellum recently offered fans an online scavenger hunt as part of the pre-release marketing for their *Own The Night* album. The contest was designed to drive awareness and also increase the trio's email list. Borman Entertainment's Cameo Carlson told *Billboard*[4] that in the fist six days of the campaign the group added 21,000 new emails to its list, increased Facebook activity by 40% and Twitter traffic by about 18%. "We're getting email addresses of fans who are really engaged," Carlson told *Billboard's* Antony Bruno. "But it's doing it in a more interesting way than just asking them to sign up for a newsletter." Carlson credited Music City Networks with developing the scavenger hunt which was designed to create deeper engagement with the band.

"We don't own anybody on Facebook or Twitter," Carlson said in the article. "Everyone has access to all these tools, but... you can't do anything with them if you don't have a relationship that's deeper than just a Facebook post. I'm always trying to figure out how to own those fans; how to convert that activity into something real."

4

http://www.billboard.biz/bbbiz/genre/country/who-says-country-music-fans-aren-t-digitally-10053304
62.story August 26, 2011, Antony Bruno "Who Says Country Music Fans Aren't Digitally Savvy? Lady Antebellum Launches Online Scavenger Hunt"

Carlson sums up exactly what this chapter is about—getting control of the data. It's great to have a social networking relationship with your consumers. But the truth is that to leverage that relationship most effectively, it is necessary to be able to contact them directly. Ultimately it means sifting through large numbers of consumers to find the ones most interested in what you have to offer and hopefully convincing them to move to ever higher levels of engagement behavior.

Chapter 3
Building Your Brand Identity In A Fragmented World Of Choice

The first step toward global online domination begins with establishing your web address. That early choice forms your digital foundation and is deserving of careful consideration.

The URL

The starting place is your URL (uniform resource locator). This is the name people will type into a web browser to find you. Securing a .com address still carries a lot of weight for most situations, because it is what people expect. You can purchase a URL at a number of online locations such as GoDaddy.com, register.com, buydomains.com and other such sites. They each have a directory search which allows you to see if the name you're hoping to find is available. Prices vary. Often times a .com address can be purchased for under $15 a year. Multi-year discounts can even lower that price. Make sure that you purchase this URL yourself, or if you have someone else involved that they list you as the owner. The URL will soon become a valuable part of your business. It's essential that you own and control it.

If you already have a company then try to find the URL that most closely matches your brand, or fits your product and/or services. A very important consideration is the length of the name. Eight letters or less is ideal. Close your eyes for a moment. What are the first few websites that come to mind? Apple, Yahoo!, AOL, Google? They all have less than six characters. I was fortunate to purchase MusicRow.com in the mid '90s which was my company's exact name and only eight letters, but short names have become increasingly hard to find.

Why do you want the shortest name possible? Because the URL (brand name) you are choosing is what people will have to type every time they look for you online or send an email to someone in your company. And, as we'll discuss shortly, it will become the basis for all your social networking accounts.

There's lots of great advice on the subject of choosing a URL. NewEntrepreneur.com[5] recommends a web address have at least three main attributes: "Short and Sim-

---

5 New Entrepreneur

http://www.newentrepreneur.com/Resources/Articles/Choosing_URL/choosing_url.html by Roger C. Parker, 2000 ple—reduce the possibility of typing errors; Descriptive—preview the content visitors will encounter; and Memorable—the best URLs combine simplicity and description with some unique element...that helps visitors remember. it."

Christopher Heng, www.thesitewizard.com[6] advises flexibility if you cannot get the domain name of your choice. "If you have an existing brand name that you're known for, you probably do not want to ditch that name just because you couldn't get the domain name," Heng says. "You might try to buy the domain name from the current owner. On the other hand, if you're just starting out, you might prefer the cheaper alternative of trying to obtain a domain name first, and then naming your website (or business) after the domain that you've acquired."

Heng is offering good advice. You can search the "whois" database, accessible on most URL purchase sites to find current URL owners, but when you contact them be prepared to pay substantially more than what a new URL might cost. Whoever owns a URL has already spent time and money developing it and may be very lukewarm about giving it up without a strong monetary incentive. Also don't get concerned if it takes a few days or weeks to pick that perfect URL. It's not unusual to end up buying several before finding a name that really feels perfect. Another word to the wise, buy the .net and .org counterparts

---

6 Tips On Choosing A Good Domain Name, Christopher Heng; 2010.
http://www.thesitewizard.com/archive/domainname.shtml

to your URL, if available. This will discourage anyone from trying to profit from your hard work after your brand becomes established. (It can be very expensive if you are forced to reclaim one of those later on, after the fact.)

Getting Social

So now you have thebrand.com and like the fabled *Goldilocks And The Three Bears,* the name is "just right." Your very next move is to reserve social networking accounts that reflect your new URL. You can start with the big three—Facebook, Twitter and YouTube. As this book is in motion, Google+ is also getting underway with brand pages, and I recommend setting that up as well.

Brand pages in Facebook and Google+ must be created from an individual account which should probably belong to the owner of the company. Facebook and Google+ then allow you to create additional "administrators" who have permission to update your company page directly from their own individual Facebook or Google+ accounts without getting access to your personal account. Twitter and YouTube are less complicated, just barge in and claim your name. For Twitter you may want to reserve a personal account and an account for your brand.

The idea is to have all the names match as closely as possible so people can easily find you. Your chosen name may not be available on all four social networks, so it will take some creativity to match them all up to each other.

Wherever possible be sure to link all the networks to each other.

"Why do I have to join so many different networks?" is a fair question. Before social networking and online connected data streams, we lived in a world of, one-thing-at-a-time. In the music industry it was vinyl recordings, then 8-tracks, then cassettes, then CDs. But today we live in a fragmented world of choices. We don't have to choose just one, we embrace many. This means that with respect to marketing, fans of your brand and potential fans, are everywhere. So it is to your advantage to be everywhere with them. Yes, there are practical considerations to administrating and updating perhaps four or more social networks plus a website. But there are also a number of shortcut tools (later chapter) that can make the process more manageable by automating a write once and post in multiple locations strategy.

The Website

Setting up your website is arguably the most time consuming and complex step in this chapter. There are a number of considerations depending upon the type of site you require, how often you are planning to update it, and your budget.

Let's start with the type of site. Websites appear to present a world of diversity, but actually most fit into two categories—the static or pamphlet site and the dynamic blog. The pamphlet site is, as the name describes something like a price list, or a printed handout. These marketing tools have a purpose, especially in print form, but they are a dead end if you want to harness *Secrets of the List* power and take advantage of today's social media-powered marketing. Yes, a pamphlet can be quite attractive and informative. But are you going to read that pamphlet year round on a daily basis? Highly unlikely. And that is the problem with the pamphlet approach. It doesn't stimulate traffic. Blog style sites, however, generally get updated on a regular basis and as a result bring readers back for return visits especially when new stories are posted to social media streams and readers are alerted with email updates.

But pamphlets do have a purpose, and it's possible, when the content dictates, to combine the two styles. A good example is the website of the Country Music Hall of Fame in Nashville. It offers museum visitors a pamphlet experience with hours of operation, how to get there, etc. But it is also updated, blog style, with articles about specific programs, speakers and more. So your first web construction decision is to decide how to best show off your brand—pamphlet, blog or both?

The second consideration is budget. Just like all other parts of running a business you need to have a realistic grasp of what you are prepared to spend in establishing your website. To this point, we have been ultra frugal in our recommendations. The URL was only a few dollars a year and signing up for Facebook, Twitter, YouTube and Google+ was free.

But trying to price a website is like car shopping, they come in many shapes, sizes and costs. I believe in letting the content speak for itself. Swirling, blinking, sliding effects, if overused, can be distracting. I like white space and an uncluttered look.

Over the past few years this writer has become a fan of open source CMS (content management system) software such as Wordpress. Wordpress allows you to download its FREE software to your host server and in minutes you have a working blog, ready to go. In addition there are hundreds of free and paid premium themes, or skins, that can be easily placed over your site in minutes to give it an original look.

After reading about Wordpress a few years ago, I leapt into starting my own blog as a test and found it to be as advertised—pretty easy. It's also easy to find a reasonably priced Wordpress developer, if you're not the DIY type. There are other open source CMS systems like Joomla and Drupal which I have heard good things about, but not used personally.

The cost of setting up a Wordpress blog (visit www.wordpress.org) might reach as high as $175 including hosting for a year. That includes purchasing a premium theme that best fits your needs which might cost from $39-$79, plus hosting space on a site such as GoDaddy which has Wordpress shared hosting plans for under $70/year. (Get hosting support or your developer to jump start your server setup.)

It is also extremely easy to move costs higher. If you woke up in the middle of the night with a vision of what your site should be, you can communicate that idea to a web development firm that will create exactly what you dreamed about, at a price! They'll work at perhaps $100/hr. or more and make your vision a reality. Creating your site this way can be great, if you can afford it. Be sure that you will be able to easily update your new site yourself. That is essential. If you continually have to pay someone to post your latest daily blog, you might start developing a severe case of writer's block brought on by cramps in your hand from writing checks.

A nice compromise for a custom site is to hire a Wordpress developer, for example, who uses WP as the base and simply programs your theme to ride on top of it all. This greatly shrinks the overall cost and insures that you get a first class CMS framework included in the bargain.

But what if you don't have even $200 to invest in a basic site at this time? There are still a few tricks you can use. In fact, you can build yourself a partially customized site for FREE! That's right. There are places online like blogger.com, wordpress.com (same software but different from wordpress.org), weebly.com, Tumblr.com and others. Most include hosting and a variety of free themes, widgets and other toys to help you create a great starter site. One drawback in this example is that your URL can be a bit long, for example http://yourcompany.tumblr.com. However, with Tumblr and Wordpress and some of the others, for a small monthly fee you can use your exact URL as the site's address. This might be a great alternative. My favorite in this space is Tumblr which is extremely customizable and viral in nature. As you study these cool web alternatives, just be sure that whichever one you choose allows you to have a signup window to capture visitor email addresses.

To put this chapter in perspective it seems sensible to ask, "What exactly is the brand, and why are we giving it a site and placing it on so many social media pages?"

Wikipedia says[7], "Brand awareness refers to customers' ability to recall and recognize the brand under different conditions and link the brand name, logo, jingles to certain associations in memory. Top-of-Mind Awareness occurs when your brand is what pops into a consumer's mind when asked to name brands in a product category."

"There is no point in dragging all your users to one point," says Forums.com Community Development Manager Bebleena Bose[8]. "The crowd can never think alike. So go out in the web as much as you can. Spread like a wildfire...and place your brand where the people are."

Establishing your online identity may be a humble beginning, but later on it will have a major impact on your brand building and on profits. The fun is in the building

---

7 http://en.wikipedia.org/wiki/Brand

8 7 Sizzling Tips to Enhance Your Online Brand Identity, Debleena Bose, Community Development Manager at Forums.com.
http://www.quickonlinetips.com/archives/2011/02/enhance-online-brand-identity/

and making new friends, lot's of new friends... So let's get started!

Chapter 4
A Garden Full Of Carrots

A dictionary search for "carrot" yields: "An offer of something enticing as a means of persuasion (often contrasted with the threat of something punitive or unwelcome). [ORIGIN: with allusion to the proverbial encouragement of a donkey to move by enticing it with a carrot.]"

Most of us learn the carrot lesson early in life, because our parents used it to get us to do things. Young children respond pretty well to this psychology, but as they get older, they begin to realize that they too, have some leverage. Leverage leads to negotiation. "Yes, I'm willing to cooperate, but I want something in return."

Most internet users are old enough to understand all three terms—carrot, leverage *and* negotiation. As a result, if you expect to attract their support you must be willing to offer something in return. Marketer Seth Godin[9] in his brilliant book *Permission Marketing* (written in 1999) understood that interactive technology would have multiple

---

9 Permission Marketing: Turning Strangers Into Friends and Friends Into Customers, writer: Seth Godin. Simon & Schuster ©1999

business implications including increased competition. As a result of the online marketplace, he wrote, "Many marketers are finding their products commoditized and their margins squeezed." But he also realized that business could use this interaction to its advantage by engaging "...its consumer customers in individual dialogues, [and] developing relationships with each of them that grow stronger with time."

The Internet has created a world of infinite shelf space. If you visit your local Wal-Mart or Kroger supermarket each store has a limited amount of area to stock and display items for sale. As a result, suppliers must fight for those limited positions which place them in front of the consumers. The Internet creates a different dynamic. Space is unlimited, because products are stacked on virtual shelves. What's scarce is consumer time and attention span. People have 24 hours each day to pay attention—and for most of us, substantially less. Building a successful consumer/brand relationship with each consumer necessitates *earning* their attention. If you can continue to gain someone's attention, that connection will ultimately build brand loyalty.

The web is littered with Top 10 articles about how to engage, cajole and influence, but what is really needed is to fully understand *your* consumer. The importance of getting to know this group cannot be overstated. The better you understand the likes and dislikes of your brand's audience the more effective you can be in trying to create a successful carrot that will motivate them to spend more time with you.

For example, what is the best way to get your potential consumers to sign up for your email news? Should you construct a contest where they must sign up to enter? What kind of prize will make them want to enter? Or will you get better results by offering each person something, like a free music download, a discount coupon or a pdf report? Asking yourself these kinds of questions will ultimately help you obtain better results.

Fortunately, there are many ways to track information that can help you better understand the habits, likes and dislikes of your users. Probably the most well known of these tools is Google Analytics which when hooked up to your website shows a wealth of information about what visitors are doing. What articles are people clicking on the most? Which ones are being ignored? As the "keeper of the brand," it is your duty to study these trails and use them to fine-tune your audience understanding.

When you send a message you become the center of a wheel and each person on your list a separate spoke. The technology allows you to measure each spoke's behavior with regard to opening the email and/or clicking on a links. This one-to-one nature of the online medium allows you to study each recipient's response to your ideas and various carrots. To build an audience you must engage them and win their loyalty. But that is only possible after you understand who they are, their values and what motivates them.

There are times in life when you get credit just for showing up. But as Brian Solis wrote in an article for Mashable.com,[10] just being there [on social media] is not enough, you must create a presence which grows based upon the sum of your engagement decisions. "Any business can join and create a profile," says Solis. "It's the devices we employ, the intentions that motivate engagement, and the value we offer that dictate the significance of the brand-specific social graphs we weave."

Solis lists 21 "Rules of Engagement," but of particular importance for this discussion is the following: "Don't just participate solely in your own domains (Facebook Fan Page, Twitter conversations related to your brand, etc.). Participate where your presence is advantageous and mandatory."

This advice harkens back to the young lemonade stand entrepreneur mentioned in the previous chapter. "Location, location, location" is most often associated with buying real estate, but it applies equally to business. If you want to grow your enterprise, you have to get in front of more potential customers. For the young entrepreneur, a lemonade stand in front of your house may be the only option, but in the virtual world there are limitless opportunities. It's fine to maintain your site and regularly update

---

10 21 Rules For Social Media Engagement, Brian Solis; Mashable.com 5/18/2010.
http://mashable.com/2010/05/18/rules-social-media-engagment/

your Twitter, Facebook, YouTube and Google+ pages and then wait for people to discover you. This steady consistency will yield results over time. But if you get out and spread the word it can accelerate your growth process. Visit a travel or recipe blog, somewhere with people that might also be a good match for your brand. Become a genuine part of its community. This means not just interrupting the blog community with a commercial message like "buy something from me," but adding to the discussion with meaningful dialogue. In this way you are moving your store to another location and putting your brand in front of new prospects that might be interested in the services and products you provide.

How else can you get your message in front of additional prospects? The traditional answer of course would be—advertise using radio, print or TV. However, a more precise approach can be to use Facebook or Google ads where you can target your message to reach people who have expressed interest in the key areas you specify. Online advertising can be cost effective, especially if you carefully aim your pitch by using "keywords" that generate results.

Google explains its adwords process in its help publication titled, *Growing Your Business With AdWords--Follow Our Tips And Watch Your AdWords Account Flourish*[11]. "Each campaign should focus on a specific product range or area of your business and then each ad group should be even

---

11 Growing Your Business With Adwords; Google;
www.google.com/adwords/pdf/hc/growing_adwords_en.pdf

more specific and focus on a subcategory of the main campaign topic," the report says. "For example, if you are a garden centre you could have a campaign focused on roses and then the ad groups (or subcategories) within that campaign could be different types of roses such as scented roses, climbing roses etc. Take inspiration from the structure of your website when deciding what campaigns and ad groups to create. Look at how you've structured your site and reflect this in your AdWords account."

Search advertising is a lot different than placing a print ad in the local weekly shopper magazine. It requires experimentation and practice to best profit from its use. To help measure your success and learn from mistakes, Google offers a suite of AdWords statistics tools.

Clickthrough Rate (CTR): How often people click on your ad after seeing it. As a rule of thumb, a CTR on Google under 1% indicates that your ads are not targeted to a relevant audience.

Keyword Status: The status column will give you more detail on your individual keyword performance.

Average Position: There are up to 11 ads shown on any search page. If your average position is 11 or higher your ad is probably not appearing on the first page of search results. You should aim to show your ad on the first page of search results so your potential customers can more easily find it.

First Page Bids: A first page bid is the cost-per-click you need to set to get your ad showing on the first page of search results.

Quality Score: Each of your keywords is given a quality score...Google rewards relevant, quality advertising with a higher position on the search page and lower costs, so making sure your ads are high quality is really important.

Facebook (search: Facebook ads) also offers a sophisticated ad buying experience. In its online ad materials the social media giant says, "Target the right people. Think about the profiles (timelines) of the people you want to reach with your ads, and select criteria based on what your audience is interested in, instead of what they might be looking to buy.

"You can target by:

-- Location, Language, Education, or Work;

-- Age, Gender, Birthday, and Relationship Status;

-- Select Likes & Interests such as camping, hiking, or backpacking instead of tents or campers;

-- Friends of Connections; and Connections."

Facebook advertisers can decide to pay on a cost per click (CPC), cost per thousand impressions (CPM) and/or specify their budget limit. The above parameters are easily set so you can choose for example to reach women age 25-35, living within 50 miles of New York City with college degrees who like boating.

Like Google, Facebook also offers detailed metrics to help you judge how your ad is doing and discover if there are ways to improve its performance.

A carefully orchestrated online ad campaign will help your brand reach potential customers, drive awareness and grow its fan base. However, it should not be confused with the carrot that is described earlier in this chapter. Why? Because after you get new faces to visit your site you still have to engage, motivate and find ways to interest them. If you fail to connect, then, like an unimpressed house hunter at a Sunday afternoon open house, your visitor will leave in search of other more attractive properties.

Get your house ready before you begin an ad campaign. Most people will not return if they arrive and find an unsatisfactory experience. Don't open up your wallet for advertising until you are sure that have something to show off.

So how much time should it take to handle the tasks briefly outlined in this chapter? According to Michael A. Stelzner's *2011 Social Media Marketing Report*[12], "Social media marketing takes a lot of time: The majority of marketers (58%) are using social media for 6 hours or more each week, and more than a third (34%) invest 11 or more hours weekly. 15% of those surveyed are spending more than 20 hours per week." Stelzner's research surveyed 3,300 marketers and found that Facebook (92%), Twitter

12 2011 Social Media Marketing Report by Michael A. Stelzner. ©2011 Social Media Examiner.
http://www.socialmediaexaminer.com/social-media-marketing-industry-report-2011/

(84%), LinkedIn (71%) and blogs (68%) were the top four social media tools used by marketers.

Perhaps most important from this study is the question of results. "A significant 88% of all marketers indicated that their social media efforts have generated more exposure for their businesses," says Stelzner. "Improving traffic and subscribers was the second major benefit, with 72% reporting positive results." Almost 70% of those polled also said that social media marketing had improved their site's search rankings which generated added exposure, new leads and a decrease in marketing expenses overall. The report also found that most respondents had less than one year of social media marketing experience.

In summary, audience building is part art and part craft. If you pay attention, over time you will learn to listen carefully to your customers. This is critical for social media engagement, but actually it has always been critical to operating a successful business. What's new is the one-on-one digital context which speeds the brand/consumer learning process. One thing remains the same, good entrepreneurs have always tried to earn and maintain their customers' loyalty and respect.

Chapter 5
List Building—
If It Was Easy,
Everyone Would
Do It!

By now you are hopefully beginning to see how the "List" strategy for online marketing can work.

1.) Engage as large a group of people as possible on social networks such as Facebook, Twitter, YouTube, Tumblr, LinkedIn and Google+;

2.) Get permission to communicate with them on a regular basis by building an email list that is created via a sign up offer on your brand's website;

3.) As a result of your skilled and genuine connection with each person via your website, social networks and regular email newsletters, your brand becomes top of mind to each person on your list and they become a loyal, revenue producing customer.

Simple. So what's the catch? Truthfully, there are a number of hurdles and skills that must be learned to maximize your results. For example, communicating with and engaging your crowd will be a challenging and complex task requiring trial and error. Where are the best places to find people with a high chance of being interested in your services or goods? Looked at another way, it's like asking where's the best fishing hole to drop your line? Are there certain social networks that have a stronger appeal to your potential crowd? These are ongoing hurdles which must be addressed one day at a time. But maybe the most frustrating aspect of direct online marketing is the start. Why?

Small companies, perhaps like yours, begin online every day with one common thread. They start with no friends, followers, circles, etc. Sounds lonely, right? It is. And it can be daunting. You're psyched to turn on the loyalty, branding and (hopefully) revenue streams, but you only have 23 people signed up. So you throw your hands up in despair and ask rhetorically, "How is this ever going to make a difference?" Well, as an Australian friend of mine says, "If it was easy, everyone would do it." At this early stage you need one crucial ingredient to separate you from the crowd: patience.

Is this some kind of backpedaling or caveat where your author quietly slips behind a curtain and leaves you wondering if this book was worth your time to read (let alone buy?) No. Rest assured my commitment to your success has not wavered. But you must realize that it takes time to develop critical mass with an engaged audience. Over time, your reach will expand until it becomes capable of helping you obtain the results you desire (and expect.) As you have no doubt realized, this chapter is about starting and growing that all-important list.

Think of this process as akin to planting a garden. After you plant the seeds, there is a period of time where it seems like nothing is happening. Regardless, you must continue watering the soil and keeping watch over the field. And then one day green shoots appear. Same thing with social networking. It starts slowly. Over time the growth pace accelerates. At first, your new page, website etc. dangles in cyber space, and no one seems to know about it. Some people will wander across it from search engines or other random activities, but if you just wait for a crowd it could take lifetimes to gather a large group. How can you speed up this process?

You have list assets at your fingertips that can act like accelerators. For example, take a look and see how many contacts you have in your email program. I just looked in my Gmail account and found 686 contacts. Letting your contacts/friends know about your new endeavor can be a great place to start. Send them a carefully crafted note. Invite them to visit your site and sign up. It's a numbers game. If, for example, your list increases 2% per week and you have 50 followers that is an increase of one person. But if you have 1,000 then your list increases by 20. As your group gets larger, the growth accelerates.

After sending out a note to your contacts, what's next? Do you have a partner? Is there anyone else in your office who might allow you to send your email to their contacts? And what about your friends and/or family? If you already have personal social networking accounts then be sure to post repeatedly about your new page and give people reasons to come visit. With a little data wrangling, you should be able to send out a wave of emails to well over a 1,000 addresses. Not everyone will take the time to click and see what you have created, but make sure, for the ones that do, that this first impression is a positive one. As said earlier in this book, say "Thanks." One simple way is to create an auto-responder that will be sent to new opt-in list subscribers saying you appreciate their interest. Mailing houses like MailChimp or Emma make this process easy to set up.

Another way to jumpstart your online voyage is to advertise via Facebook and/or Google. As discussed in Chapter 4, these messages can be highly targeted and help speed the process. Acquiring those first 100 names can seem like an eternity. But after that it gets better.

For example, I first created a *MusicRow* magazine Twitter account on Sept. 19, 2008. Most people hardly knew what it was at that time, but it seemed interesting to me. It took weeks just to get 30 followers. The company that owned *MusicRow* at the time, SouthComm, had several publications and we were the only one on Twitter. I remember reporting to a group of executives at a company board meeting that we had 43 followers. No one was especially impressed, and for that matter, they had no idea why it might ever become important. Today (2/10/2012), *Musi-*

cRow has almost 32,800 followers, a pretty large number for a trade magazine. We tweet headlines with links to each article we publish online. You'd be surprised how much traffic that process generates for the publication's website. Of course the increased traffic has also translated nicely into ad dollars!

The focus of this book is virtual, but that doesn't mean we should ignore real world strategies. Are you interacting with customers daily? Maybe they are coming into your store, or you have sales people that go out to visit them? Plan ways to make customers aware of your online initiatives with a carrot to help them remember. Your virtual addresses should be on every printed item you create such as business cards, notepads and/or stationary.

You can find many sites and authors offering list building techniques. A lot of what you will find is uninspired, but ideas have a way of stimulating other ideas. Sometimes even the same thought expressed slightly differently can spark progress.

Marketer Stella Anokam, a Consulting/Project Management executive has a blog with a number of marketing articles. One, for example, is titled, "Top 10 Strategies To Get More Visitors To Become Your List Subscribers[13]."

"The money is in big, fat lists," says Anokam. "And that brings us to the question, 'How big is your list? Is your list growing day by day?'" The principle behind list building

---

13 "Top Ten Effective List Building Strategies To Increase Your Subscriber Base" by Stella Anokam.
http://www.stellaanokam.com/get-more-subscribers-effective-strategies-2576

she states is, "...casting your net wide and far, in order to help more of your target audience find and reach you fast..."

Anokam suggests, "Ask yourself: Can your readers truly use the tips in any and every one of your posts to solve a single problem? If they use your DIY tips and see results, they'll like and trust you and they'll want to stick real close – by subscribing."

This is good advice. Stick close to your field of expertise and show readers that you really know what you are doing. Giving them actionable articles to solve a specific problem is a strong way to make an impression.

This idea can also be expanded upon. In addition to an article, and depending upon your area of expertise, you might offer a free downloadable report, or a free song if you are an artist. The more helpful the item, the stronger the pull of the carrot and the faster your list will grow.

MailChimp offers an instructive example of a company giving its customers DIY advice that inspires trust and confidence. At http://mailchimp.com/resources/ you will find a library of about 25 short reports on using MailChimp and getting the most out of e-mail. Each one is downloadable in three formats, (pdf, epub and mobi) making them compatible with a wide range of e-readers and other devices. Some of the titles include "Email Security," "How To Manage Your List," "Spam Lawsuits," "MailChimp For Bloggers," "MailChimp For Musicians" and more. Let's look inside the one named, "How To Create An Email Marketing Plan."

"Current research suggests that email marketing is among the most cost-effective marketing tactics available," states the MailChimp report. "For example, the Ad Effectiveness Survey commissioned by *Forbes Media* in Feb./March 2009 reveals that email and e-newsletter marketing is considered the second most effective tool for generating conversions (that means customers)—just behind Search Engine Optimization." Spread out over ten pages, this report walks the new user through a simple process (and non-technical) of creating an email campaign. "Define your audience," it begins. "Once you define the group or groups you want to send to...jot down a few bullet points to help define them a little more. Maybe a few key words that describe the people in the group and what the group will want to get out of your campaign."

Referencing the people that have signed up to receive your list the report says, "Honor this group of dedicated customers and fans. Give them access to special benefits as subscribers such as useful tips and tricks, special offers and exclusive coupons. Maybe even give them special insight into your company so they feel like they are getting to know you on a personal level." As added advice it tells users to be brief and show some personality, "the email newsletter format is less formal than a print article or brochure." Lastly, this MailChimp guide says to "Outline your goals, determine your frequency and create a [production] timeline."

Emma.com, another newsletter service has its "Ask Emma" Q&A series. And www.constantcontact.com provides a "Learning Center, where questions meet answers." The point is that each service has seen the need and the benefits from providing tips, tricks and help to its users.

The list, the list, the list...it's all about the list. But building this new tool will not happen overnight and it simply can't be rushed. That means it's worth repeating something said at the beginning of this chapter, "You need one crucial ingredient to keep you going—PATIENCE."

Think of yourself as a settler coming to a new land to build a city. It starts with just a tent for yourself, then you build a stronger more useful shelter of wood and stone. Ultimately more people arrive and decide to stay. Families develop and the population explodes. Little by little roads are built connecting to other locations and with each improvement the young city grows taller, stronger and larger. Starting a direct marketing list can make you feel like those early settlers. You have a vision, a belief that others will find what you are doing useful. But the gains are slow at first. Stay focused and continue to believe.

How much time you should spend on the list, your emails, website and social media posts depends upon a lot of factors—the most important of which is your schedule. Try to post something daily on the key social networks (at least Twitter and Facebook). Link to news stories from other sites that are relevant to your audience. In Chapter 6 we get into specific ways to build content for your website.

When you post to your website, be sure to share your article (w/links) across all your social media accounts. There are a number of tools which we will discuss in a later chapter that help accomplish this task by allowing you to write once and post to all. A better strategy is to post twice a day. Research shows that mid-morning and late afternoon are high visibility times. Be consistent. Don't be afraid to share your content a second time on social media. Simply rewrite your comments a bit.

Don't feel like a failure because you haven't set everything up at once; website, email signup, newsletter frequency, social network accounts plus written extensive tips and tricks reports. Start with the social networks. Signup takes little or no time and you can begin building your community right away. The other pieces, like the framework for a giant city can be added one at a time.

Congratulations on getting this far into this book. I hope you're enjoying it. By the way, have you gotten a URL and set up your social media accounts yet? What are you waiting for? Get started now!

Chapter 6
Home Base—Your Brand's Website

Like a finely tuned race car, where the mechanical systems are lovingly blended into perfect balance in order to win a race, a branding regimen also needs its various elements working together harmoniously. For example, imagine what might happen to a brand with a great social networking presence, which successfully engages friends and followers and motivates them to visit the brand's website. But suppose that upon arrival to the website they are disappointed, find little of interest and instead of signing up to receive the newsletter, they depart—confused, and feeling that the brand was not deserving of their trust and/or passion.

This scenario would be the definition of an online marketing disaster. Another possible problem might be the beautifully conceived website, which lacks effective implementation because it was simply too ambitious considering the resources that were available to run it.

In Chapter 3 we discussed some of the basic considerations for website concepting. You'll recall we briefly divided most websites into content, pamphlet or hybrid models. We also pointed out the importance of being able to stimulate visitors to return regularly.

The content site requires constant updating. It has an insatiable appetite for new stories and details. The pamphlet is exactly the opposite. Once finished, like a printed page, the copy remains untouched for long periods of time or until something about the company changes like the hours of operation, or a new product offering. Finally the hybrid uses elements from both the above examples to produce a site with more balance which often times can be successful without demanding massive time and resources.

Visualizing your website's look and feel can be daunting, but paying attention to the kinds of content and what is required to produce and update that content is where the races are won and lost. Website design is a lot less important than content. In fact, in most cases less is truly more with respect to design. You certainly don't want your content getting drowned out by massive backgrounds and vision sapping color saturation. To help illustrate this point go visit a few [or lots] of your favorite sites. News sites like the *Wall Street Journal,* the *New York Times, CNN* and many others reserve bright colors and blinking/flashing mostly just for advertisers. The site's are built around white space with photos. Be on the lookout for good ideas that you can borrow for your new site.

All content is not equal when it comes to its creation. For example, original articles require more work than lists and feeds which update automatically. Let's take a look at some content ideas and possible usages for all three types of sites—content, pamphlet and hybrid.

The Widget

The Internet is loaded with widgets, [thankfully]. Wikipedia[14] says, "A widget is a stand-alone application that can be embedded into third party sites by any user on a page where they have rights of authorship (e.g. a webpage, blog, or profile on a social media site). Widgets allow users to turn personal content into dynamic web apps that can be shared on websites where the code can be installed. For example, a 'Weather Report Widget' could report today's weather by accessing data from the Weather Channel, it could even be sponsored by the Weather Channel. Should you decide to put that widget on your own site, you could do this by copying and pasting the embed code."

Widgets, such as the weather or stock market prices will fluctuate on a steady basis and are great for content, pamphlet and hybrid sites. They continually update and refresh, generating new content on a regular basis. Think of the widget's role as being something like a holiday stocking stuffer. It's probably not a big enough gift to motivate

---

14 http://en.wikipedia.org/wiki/Web_widget

people to visit frequently, but it helps to give the impression that a site is busy, informative and up to date.

When planning your website's content agenda, a good beginning is to list the widgets that might make sense to include. Some of these things are automatic. If you are on Twitter, Facebook, Google Plus and YouTube you will probably want to include a widget from each social network. Facebook, for example has several different kinds of widgets. One—Facepile—shows how many "Likes" your page has, plus offers constantly changing photos from some of your fans. Twitter allows you to design the colors and even the content of one of its best widgets which places a steady stream of updates, either from just yourself, or including mentions.

Widgets are often branded with advertising, but still qualify as content. Because they provide updates automatically and require little or no effort from the website owner they fit nicely on both content and pamphlet sites. The other obvious benefit is they provide clear unmistakable signposts directing visitors to your social network properties and other important destinations. Not everyone will enter your "brand world" via a social network. Suppose someone arrives first at your website? In that case, you want to make sure they know about enjoying all your brand's other engagement entities and are only a click away from visiting them.

Pamphlet Site

A purely pamphlet-style site is essentially a static, unchanging digital wasteland. Think of it as a dead end street. There is much to be learned from studying pamphlet-style content however, because ultimately, like a digital chef, you can mix it with dynamic content.

Pamphlet data includes things like Where to Find Us, Hours of Operation, Products, Prices and more. We are talking about information which rarely changes. Suppose you were taking a trip to a nearby city to visit a tourist attraction. It would make perfect sense for you to check out the attraction's website to find out exactly when it was open and how much a ticket will cost. After you get that information, and view a few photos, you are done. Chances are you will not return to that site again unless you are planning a second trip a few months later.

What a wasted opportunity for the brand. You were there, eager to participate, but the brand elected to give you a few static facts and send you away. What if they offered you a chance to get discounts by signing up for an email newsletter? What if there were current articles on the site related to the brand experience? What if there were comments from other visitors with opinions and thoughts on their visits? What if they asked you to Like their Facebook page and Follow them on Twitter?

The possibilities were endless, but this brand missed out on most of them simply because they weren't ready or just didn't care. A visitor entered their digital storefront to find out information, but there was nothing to engage them. Maybe they wouldn't participate in every offering—Twitter, Facebook, email list and more. But they might have opted in on at least one. Every click that adds to a consumer's relationship with the brand is worth something.

Dynamic Content

Original, high quality content is like fine wine, it can't be rushed and it takes time to create. There are many different kinds of articles, interviews, editorials, reviews and more which qualify for the "original" badge. With respect to engagement potential, original data can be very powerful. A single article, video clip or interview can stimulate page views and comments and fuel a viral click-fest that brings lots of traffic to a website and highly engages your visitors. Of course not every article will achieve a viral response, but when compared with static data, quality dynamic content is like rocket fuel vs. water.

So why not just use 100% high octane fuel, i.e. original content on your brand's site? The first reason is because to generate originality on a regular basis requires talented writers and thinkers and they cost time and money. So there are budget considerations to address. Some static info is not only expected, it is demanded. What if you visited the tourist attraction site in our above example and couldn't find the hours of operation? That would be frustrating.

Sometimes your company has original content that it is already producing for another purpose. At *MusicRow* magazine when we were first creating our company website some of the information we used came from information we were already compiling. For example, we were keeping a calendar of upcoming single and album artist releases and realized it would translate perfectly into the digital environment and be of use to our readers. Our weekly radio charts were another source of updated content that we were already producing on a weekly basis.

Your company has some data of this type which it is already creating. Perhaps it is the results of weekly research or maybe even a ranking of the company's best sales items each week. Sometimes it can even be information that suggests the size and scope of the company's operations. For example, a weekly chart showing the sum total of miles driven by all company delivery vehicles each week. Do not overlook these kinds of data. They can provide value and are relatively inexpensive to transfer online.

Hybrid Recipe

Finally, like a gourmet food engineer who has carefully assembled his ingredients (widgets, pamphlet data and dynamic data) we sit down to create our culinary, or in this case digital masterpiece. In addition to the actual blend of ingredients there are other considerations such as the cost and time involved in preparing the dish, er... website.

Simply stated we want a blend of the three above named items, done in such a way that it delivers maximum impact and engagement for our visitors without becoming too expensive to maintain.

The first part of a good website recipe consists of preparing the static data. Take time to create a complete list of everything which visitors might need to know regarding your brand. Special kinds of brands might have additional info items in this category. For example, if you make snack cakes perhaps visitors want to know the products' nutritional values.

After the static data has been curated, it is time to consider the size and scope of your commitment to original data. This is tricky to balance properly against available resources. If you are a small business, will you be doing these articles yourself? When will you do them? Perhaps you plan to hire a full time Community Manager to create original content for your website, post to your social networks, answer questions and generally be involved in the basic conversation and engagement activities. These thoughts should be part of your decision. Don't forget that visitor feedback is also a form of original content. Ask them to upload a photo of themselves using your product or something similar. User content can be extremely engaging and sticky once it catches on. (All data does double duty by being post-able on your social networks with links back to your site.)

Now that you have blended static and dynamic content into a tasty mix, what remains is to fold in a few eye-catching widgets to add some visual spice. Obvious first choices here will be widgets and/or badges that connect with the social networks and link to your brand's pages on those networks. Personally, I love the ones that feature your Likes, Followers, etc. in some way. Other widgets should have some kind of relationship to your brand.

The online space is constantly changing and evolving. Therefore it is permissible and acceptable for your website to reflect this trait. Do not feel that you are required to dip your first content recipe in concrete and never change it. On the contrary, visitors will enjoy seeing it evolve over time. However, as discussed at the start of this chapter, it is critical to always do your best to successfully engage your visitors. Don't over promise and under deliver. Strive for balance. If the brand's social networking properties and website reflect the same integrity and a unified message then you are on your way to building a successful direct marketing presence and reaping its benefits.

Chapter 7
The Laws of The Digital Jungle

Dictionary.com defines "Law of the Jungle" as "a system or mode of action in which the strongest survive, presumably as animals in nature or as human beings whose activity is not regulated by the laws or ethics of civilization."

If you were walking in the jungle you would take precautions to avoid becoming the main course on some large predator's dinner table. You'd also stay away from a city's late night dark alleys where trouble might be lurking. Even young Boy Scouts train to "Be Prepared," and that's good advice. In the same way, recognizing some of the basic traits of the Internet can go a long way toward making better online marketing decisions. But how can you evaluate all the conflicting warnings and promises?

Remarkably, many people venture online daily, giving little or no thought to how the digital world works. They just grab their mouse and go. On all sides, we hear people telling us what to look out for and how they are going to fix problems such as spam emails, pirated intellectual property, identity theft, Digital Rights Management and much more. Interested parties promote legislative bills aimed at righting the wrongs and fixing what's broken. But how does one apply a realistic yardstick to these problems and supposed solutions?

One surefire way to become better informed is to observe how the Internet is constructed—what I like to refer to as the "Laws of the Digital Jungle."

Law #1: All Digital Locks Can Be Broken

There are several "Laws of the Digital Jungle." Perhaps the hardest to grasp is the idea that, "All Digital Locks Can Be Broken." The Internet was designed to distribute information under adverse conditions. Online data doesn't travel in a straight line, it flows along various pathways like a giant spider web. If one strand breaks, the info immediately chooses the next fastest route to its destination.

Howstuffworks.com[15] has numerous articles explaining technical details about web science. Here is an edited paragraph that explains how web data gets broken into packets and then sent along numerous routes to its destination.

"Every Web page that you receive comes as a series of packets, and every e-mail you send leaves as a series of packets. Networks that ship data around in small packets

---

15 "What is a packet?" 01 December 2000. HowStuffWorks.com.
http://computer.howstuffworks.com/question525.htm 14 January 2012.

are called packet switched networks...Each packet carries the information that will help it get to its destination—the sender's IP address, the intended receiver's IP address, something that tells the network how many packets this e-mail message has been broken into and the number of this particular packet...Each packet is then sent off to its destination by the best available route—a route that might be taken by all the other packets in the message or by none of the other packets in the message. If there is a problem with one piece of equipment in the network while a message is being transferred, packets can be routed around the problem, ensuring the delivery of the entire message."

Baked into the very DNA of a packet switched network is the dedication to information reaching its destination. The Internet is porous, more like a screen door than a steel wall and therefore data will permeate it thoroughly. This spreading of information also has the effect of making it possible to defeat software that tries to set up data roadblocks—commonly known as digital rights management. A quick internet search for "hacking competition" will locate numerous stories about companies that challenged the Internet community to break into their carefully planned, "totally secure," info vaults. As you'll see, the hackers win every time.

Just because hacking can be done doesn't mean that everyone at home has the capability to do these kinds of sophisticated programming exploits, some folks argue. True, but one can be assured that if a strong consumer incentive is created, then complex ways to open these locks will be simplified for ordinary users. An interesting current-day example is the ability to unlock smartphones. I could never accomplish this totally on my own, but there are instructional videos on YouTube and easily found step-by-step tutorials which detail how to "jailbreak" or unlock whatever smartphone you own.

The take-away here is that you will get better results using the carrot than the stick. (See Chapter 4: A Garden Full Of Carrots.) Incentivise your community to follow, do not try to force them. Give them a compelling reason to follow your lead.

The music industry is a classic example of an industry that did not understand that all digital locks can be broken. Peer-2-Peer file sharing network Napster threatened the industry in 2000, having amassed 60 million active users who were sharing music illegally. The labels chose to deal with this new technology through litigation instead of partnering and trying to monetize it. After shutting Napster down, their second step was to try and lock all the music using digital rights management. Today the labels have given up on DRM, admitting it didn't work. In the process they alienated customers. Today, sales have dropped over 50% from 2000 and the number of major labels continues to shrink.

In August 2007, a think tank collaboration at my home with songwriter Jim Beavers, and futurists David Gales, Scott Heuerman and Todd Cassetty produced "Embracing Change—The New Rules Of Engagement." The Special

Report was aimed at helping the music industry adjust and adapt. Here's an edited excerpt, from the foreword to the report titled "The Digital Age: A Brief History[16]." It attempts to sum the issues of digital locks, DRM and employing the carrot vs. the stick while blaming the industry's problems on the imaginary and mysterious character, Lord Digital—creator of the MP3.

"Once upon a time, years ago, the music was locked up behind bricks and mortar. Labels controlled where, when and how consumers were able to access it. Then came the Internet and the rise to power of the mysterious Lord Digital. Soon afterwards the digital lord spawned MP3, and in so doing, cleverly cemented his control over music in the Internet domain.

"Labels soon felt the disruptive power of MP3. The distribution locks were broken forever, and the music business model which was producing great wealth began to unravel. But the labels remained steadfast in denial and responded by choosing litigation as a means to suppress change and fight the growing wave of illegal downloads.

"Unit sales tumbled, but industry gurus called it 'another cycle.' Label advisors recommended Digital Rights Management promising, 'It will return everything to normal.' Regrettably, DRM didn't improve business, but it did make fans angry. Sales got worse, revenues continued

---

16 *Embracing Change—The New Rules Of Engagement; by David Ross, Jim Beavers, David Gales, Scott Heuerman and Todd Cassetty. ©MusicRow 2007.*
http://www.musicrow.com/wp-content/uploads/2009/07/newrulesfinal.pdf. The Digital Age: A Brief History, Foreword by David M. Ross.

dropping and mass merchandisers demanded to sell the music at lower prices to boost demand. It became clear that new rules of engagement were needed to channel Lord Digital's power and re-establish prosperity and peace."

Law #2: Supply & Demand Needs Scarcity

The second law of the digital jungle reaffirms a basic real world economic principle: The relationship between pricing and the laws of supply and demand. Simply stated, when the supply is low and the demand high, prices rise. Conversely, an abundance of supply with weak demand will cause prices to drop.

This principle seems reliable in the real world, dealing with physical widgets. However, the digital world does not always adhere to this maxim. Why? It's all about scarcity. In the digital environment and especially with intellectual property, it is difficult or impossible to enforce the necessary ingredient for controlling supply—scarcity.

The movie, book and music industries are still learning the painful lesson that in the digital world they have much less control over distribution and therefore pricing. When a consumer has the option to get the files for free from a pirate website, that constitutes unlimited supply, implies zero scarcity and therefore forces a rethinking of pricing strategy. A seller forced to compete with free (stealing), is in a dangerous and unpleasant position from which to operate. However, the battle can still be won by offering better access, choice and ease of use and taking advantage of lowered costs. Pricing in such a situation needs to be considered as a volume proposition. If prices are placed too high, then the consumer will be pulled toward free, like a moth to a flame.

Law #3: Consumer Behavior Can't Be Legislated

This last axiom may be hard to prove conclusively, although my observations over the past decade strongly support it. Consumers are not perfect creatures, but given a reasonable value proposition, they will endeavor to do the right thing. That is to say they will not steal, if you can give them a compelling alternative. However, when government or a company tries to limit or derail a new technology, they most often find themselves standing dangerously in the pathway of a speeding train.

Matrix fans will remember the nefarious Agent Smith forcibly holding Mr. Anderson (Neo) in the pathway of an approaching train. "Do you hear that train Mr. Anderson?" says Smith menacingly. "That is the sound of your death, the sound of inevitability." Neo escaped at the last minute, but if you play chicken with the technology train, you may not be so lucky. Trying to keep consumers from embracing new opportunities is bad business. A safer strategy (and more fun) is to get on board, ride the train and sell tickets.

Business concerns sometimes lobby the government for a legislative answer to their online problems. Unfortunately, each solution often causes additional unintended consequences. It is a mistake to use government as a force to restrict the development of new online possibilities. For example, you can pass laws against illegal file sharing and the theft of intellectual property like movies, books and music. But if legal alternatives are not available, the theft will not stop.

The digital jungle rulebook is simply saying, consumers want *what* they want, *when* they want it, and *how* they want it. If you don't find a way to make it available to them in a legal format which they find reasonable, they will get it another way. It's not always pretty, but that is the way human nature works in the digital construct. It's the law inside the digital jungle.

Chapter 8
Connecting The Dots With An Email Launch

Congratulations. You've now reached the connecting phase of your direct marketing matrix—the email newsletter. And using the term "launch" is no accident. Why? Because the email, like a rocket ship, will carry your message to new destinations setting in motion the *Brand Engagement Behavior* we discussed and illustrated with a graph in Chapter 2.

So let's review how we got here with a fast check list. Hopefully you can say "Check" aloud after reading each point.

—Established and have been updating at least a few social media accounts like Facebook and Twitter. Planning to add additional networks such as YouTube, Google+, Tumblr, Pinterest, etc.

—Purchased a URL and created a website?

—Created an email newsletter account and started a list.

—Placed a conspicuously positioned newsletter sign-up widget on your website that is connected to your email newsletter account.

—Carefully read Chapter 5 about list building and have begun finding ways to grow your list.

—Added content to the website that you hope might interest your new community.

—Followed @davidmross on Twitter and signed up for his newsletter at www.secretsofthelist.com? (This step is not essential to your success, but shows the kind of self-promotion you want to emulate.)

Well OK then, let's get started on the launch.

Get Started Now

As you have probably noticed, each of the spokes on the social media/brand engagement wheel require skills that take some time to acquire. So it is a fair question to ask, "I've got my Facebook page working pretty well, but I really haven't got my YouTube or Google+ accounts up to speed. Should I start with the email anyway?" The answer is emphatically, "YES," as long as you have your website created.

Each new piece you place on the social media chess-board becomes part of a learning process. First, it takes time to discover the basics of how it operates. Next you find through trial and error how to get the most community response. So don't wait, hoping for that magic day to arrive when a light goes on above your computer signifying that you have mastered everything. It's not going to happen. New things are being introduced all the time, and the best you can do, depending upon the time you have available, is to keep up and continue growing your list.

I've also heard people say, "My list isn't very big, maybe I should wait before starting the emails." Wrong. As soon as you have some facility with your social networks and have a site up and running it is time to begin this all-important process. Why? Because creating these emails is another rung on the ladder of your success that will also take time to perfect. You'll start to feel the benefit of the email's thrust as it draws clicks to your content.

As previously discussed, there are several good choices available to help you build and send your emails plus maintain your lists. Try searching "email html newsletters" or just "email newsletters" and you'll find many of them. MailChimp is the one I use because its interface is easy to learn and it offers a free account for lists with under 2,000 names. Just like working with each of the social networks, creating emails will get easier over time. So start right away, because most likely it will take a while to fine tune the process.

Email Content

Personally, I like the chance to engage in a personal discussion with my community, so it's not unusual for me to start the newsletter with some kind of personal message about what has been happening since the last email went out, and then highlight the new content that I'm hoping my readers/community will find interesting. I know it's unlikely that every reader will find every article irresistible. That's OK. Hopefully, there will be something they will want to click on. And you can be building a relationship even if it's just because you took a moment to connect with a warm "hello," a pat on the back, or an "I understand what you are going through." But be sincere. For the best results make sure you genuinely relate to what you are saying. An opening "chat" also allows you to toss out subjects that might not easily fit into specific articles, but that your community might find engaging. Sometimes you discover a viral topic that spurs engagement like high-grade rocket fuel.

For example, suppose you are a company that builds and cares for outdoor swimming pools. It's an obvious choice to write about pool chemicals, swim toys and other related subjects. But suppose in your personal "chat" you said your new puppy was learning to swim and unexpectedly you get lots of questions about that? It might mean that writing an article about pets and pools would get good results.

Email content varies greatly, but you don't have much time to make an impression. Readers will likely give it a glance and perhaps focus for 10-20 seconds. Try to make sure that your biggest and best topics will be the first things they notice. An attention getting photo is also helpful. Be careful not to have all the headlines the same size. The reader's eye will move from the largest to the smallest type if you arrange the page so it flows smoothly. Have some consistency.

The kind of content you are sharing should dictate how you position it and whether it is complete or excerpted with a "click to read more" link. These decisions can actually be complex and yield quite different results. For example, Charles Schwab offers daily stock portfolio newsletters that have the closing prices for each of the holdings in a client's account. This is really more of a client service than a newsletter, although it certainly reinforces brand engagement, too. But what if they sent the email and you had to click and visit the website to get each closing price? That would be more of a nuisance than a service wouldn't it?

CNN's breaking news alerts serve a different function. Most readers, want to see the headlines with maybe one or two sentences. Then they decide which stories they want to pursue and click to read the complete article on the website. CNN is engaging daily with readers on its "alerts" list, but at the same time realizes that if it sent out complete stories for each headline the size of the missive would make it all but impossible to quickly scan. The likely result would be a wave of "Unsubscribe." CNN actively sells ads on its website so the linked headline approach has the added benefit of drawing traffic back to its site, and making the ad spots more valuable.

Some newsletters are hybrid—they have click back links *and* small news blurps without links. This could accommodate long form articles and short form announcements. An electronics store, for example, might use click back links for a story about how to choose the best HD TV or set up wifi wireless Internet with a cable modem at home. But they might also want to be sure and let you know that this Saturday there will be a 40% off sale on Samsung TVs, or Friday they will host an in-store workshop.

It is also worth mentioning that there are companies that supply generic articles for dentists, dry cleaners, plumbers and perhaps your type of business. Use caution here. A few of these generic articles go a long way, meaning they rarely rank high on the engagement scale because there is little or personalization. Use them sparingly.

Allow your newsletter content decisions to develop over time. Don't demand of yourself a fully mature newsletter that rivals multi-million dollar brands on day one. But be sure to sign up for newsletters from other companies similar to yours. The old saying, "Imitation is the sincerest form of flattery," makes perfect sense in this situation. There are many good ideas out there. Often with a pinch of creativity you can rework them to fit your needs.

Look And Feel

Designing your newsletter can be a daunting task. But it doesn't have to be. Most newsletter services offer you hundreds of different templates you can personalize. MailChimp divides templates into two main groups—basic layouts and pre-designed. Study them carefully. In order to get started you must have a few content units ready to go. As discussed above, maybe it's a letter to your readers, an announcement of some kind, linked icons to your social media pages, plus a linked article headline. One of the first newsletter decisions is how many columns it will have and what the header will look like. If you think it's appropriate for your content use one of the pre-designed templates. But don't be upset if the graphical template approach falls flat. Sometimes they end up looking too much like a hobbyist blog instead of a professional business. That's OK. Experimenting is part of the learning process.

Basic layouts often yield better results. Mostly they consist of a blank header that sits atop a set number of columns. Start simple and add as you go along. Two columns works nicely because it allows you to separate the content and helps the eye to scan more topics faster without scrolling down the page. Most systems allow you to send a test email to yourself which is absolutely a good idea. See that the design matches what you were expecting and test all the links to see if they work properly.

After you send out your first email be sure to study the campaign report. In MailChimp, for example, it will show how many unique and total opens the email received, plus how many clicks were generated and by which specific links. You can even drill down and see that data broken out by recipient. You'll have a good read on your email about 24 hours after it is sent. Study the information so you can start to get a feel for the kind of content that most interests your readers.

Chapter 9
Tooling Around Online

Man's ability to invent and use tools has been one of the building blocks of civilization. We usually think of real world tools, like those used to build a house, but the virtual world also benefits from talented programmers who are finding ways to make our online lives more efficient. In fact, the lines between our analog and virtual lives are increasingly becoming blurred. (Don't you agree?)

Yes, the Internet was supposed to be a tremendous time saver, allowing us to complete tasks in shorter time and therefore increase our leisure time. Unfortunately, we all know how that turned out [not so much]. So because we are as desperately out of time as ever, we need digital tools to help us speed through the changing character of our mixed up and increasingly confused online/offline, virtual/analog, lives.

Therefore it should be no surprise that the number of social media tools is mushrooming almost as fast as the number of networks they serve. New contenders are arriving daily, each with new ways to share, post and measure information, personal taste, opinions, graphics and more.

From the standpoint of this book, there is likely no perfect way to write about this rapidly changing and important aspect of our social media lifestyle. So rather than attempt precise recommendations with detailed operating manuals, it seems more valuable to offer an overview of what tools are available now and why they might be helpful. Keep in mind that the "digital gizmo" landscape is continually evolving. What best fits your needs will depend upon the various social networking sites that you frequent, the mobile and desktop hardware you use and the kinds of content you like to post. Test drive as many of these time savers as you can to gauge how effectively each fits your needs.

Looked at as a group, the tools have different functions. They can automate the posting of content, using a post once, send to multiple sites, time-saving approach. Many have a write now-post later function which allows you to get maximum engagement by sending out information at times that best fit the reading habits of your audience. For some tools the main thrust is to track engagement metrics and measure social media growth. Lastly, some tools combine content, measurement, response tracking and time shifting. So let's take a look inside the digital toolbox...

Tweetdeck

As the name suggests this tool is closely aligned with Twitter. Earlier versions played nicely with Facebook, Facebook Pages, LinkedIn, MySpace and Foursquare. Unfortunately, the newest version (now owned by Twitter) seems to interface only with multiple Twitter and Facebook accounts. Tweetdeck offers the ability to create multiple columns so you can watch streams of Tweets, Mentions and/or specific searches pass in real time. You can post to your Facebook and/or Twitter accounts and schedule delivery. Tweetdeck is a powerful solution depending upon the types of stories you like to post. The program's main downside concerns posting news stories to Facebook. Unlike posting directly from inside Facebook with a link, or by using an article's Like button, Tweetdeck is unable to include an article's graphic when posting to Facebook—only text and a link. But for Twitter fans Tweetdeck is a must.

Share Once, Post To Multiple Networks

There are numerous apps, and checkboxes inside apps, that facilitate automatic reposting. In fact, there are so many different alternatives that it is impractical to mention them all here.

For example, if you have a Wordpress blog which publishes its RSS feed through Google Feedburner (a good idea), then you can click a Feedburner setting which takes each new RSS blog entry and auto-tweets it to whatever account you link up. A simple Twitter setting can then make sure the Tweet auto-posts to your Facebook account. Facebook can then further automate reposting to different sites.

At first auto-posting appears to be a fabulous time saver. But is it really? It depends upon what content you post and how often. Based upon the above example as you publish your blog story it automatically posts to Twitter and Facebook. But maybe the automated headline which appears on Twitter is not phrased for maximum engagement results. Could you have rewritten the tweet to produce something more interesting? Would the post have benefited on Facebook by having a visible graphic to gain attention?

As social networkers become more experienced they seem to gravitate away from trying to cover every option with one click. News publications, for example, might be comfortable auto-posting news stories from the company website to Twitter. But they are likely to post manually to Facebook, and Google Plus to insure getting the right visuals to accompany each story. Experiment and you will find the right balance to best present your material. Don't make the mistake of thinking that posting is only about quantity and speed. Yes, you should be consistent on a daily basis, but your emphasis should be upon quality. How can I stand out? What will be interesting to my followers? Remember, all content is not created equal.

Hootsuite

Hootsuite calls itself a "Social Media Dashboard." It allows one to manage multiple social network profiles, track mentions, analyze traffic, schedule tweets and create dazzling reports. A key functionality for larger companies is that it allows team management. The basic plan is Free and its Pro Plan is $5.99 per month. There is also an enterprise level. It's easy to get overwhelmed studying the home page for a product this robust. One way to speed the involvement process is to first sign up for the Free account and go exploring. After you have some idea of the terrain, visit Hootsuite's Help Desk where they have a series of articles to help complement your activities.

Crowdbooster

The name tells the story for this site, which is dedicated to boosting your social media crowd at Facebook and Twitter. Crowdbooster's press states, "Crowdbooster helps you achieve an effective presence on Twitter and Facebook. We show you analytics that aren't based on abstract scores, but numbers that are connected to your business and your social media strategies: impressions, total reach, engagement, and more. We then give you the tools and recommendations you need to take action and improve each one of these metrics." The free version limits you to one Twitter account and one Facebook Page, but gives you a taste of the site's incredible analytics and recommendations abilities. Paid upgrades are available (of course) which include more accounts and functionality.

Analytics include estimates of how many people were reached and which of your tweets got the most response. Your most influential followers are highlighted so you can be sure to interact with them on a regular basis. Follower growth gets mapped out in detail and Crowdbooster makes recommendations as to what times of the day you should schedule your tweets to reach the highest number of people. You can also send and schedule tweets directly from inside its website. This tool only recently moved out of beta, but offers an incredible wealth of information, intuitively displayed. Other newcomers in the analytics arena include PostRank (https://analytics.postrank.com), recently purchased by Google and currently in beta. It measures engagement across more than 20 top networks.

Ping.fm

Ping is like a social media Swiss Army knife, supporting over 32 different networks. Top tier supported networks include Twitter, LinkedIn, Facebook, MySpace, Tumblr and Facebook Pages. (Still missing is Google+.) You can use Ping.fm across most online platforms including web, Android and IOS. Ping's interface can be a bit buggy when trying to link to your various accounts, but most issues are solved by logging in and out of the offending network. Like Tweetdeck, Seesmic and other post-once-to-many solutions—and as discussed above in the Auto-posting section—choosing this approach means accepting a number of compromises in the look and feel of your messages on different networks.

Social Magazine Apps— Flipboard, Google Currents, Zite, Flud News, Google Reader

These apps present a robust media consumption experience, but their family roots can be traced to the humble RSS reader. Their purpose is to expose the user to a large number of articles from various sources, all inside one interface.

Flipboard, Google Currents, Zite and Flud News are some of the better known examples at this time. Each of these apps allow the reader to choose feeds and sources and then share stories as desired across most networks. They all have slightly different capabilities. The contest is to find one with an interface you enjoy, that is available for the hardware platform(s) you use and plays nicely with the network(s) you frequent.

I am including Google Reader in this grouping even though it's a pure RSS reader, not a magazine-style news delivery system. Why? Because Reader is a faster and more efficient way to read a large number of feeds than any of the magazine style, graphic-intensive options above. It also has robust sharing capabilities. For smartphone users, it also requires less bandwidth and battery which can save money if your mobile carrier charges for data overages.

Klout.com

Is Klout a social network or an analytics outpost? Probably a little of both. Whatever name you assign, it's lots of fun. To get started connect your Twitter, FB and

Google+ networks. Secondary accounts such as YouTube, Foursquare, LinkedIn and a few others are optional. Klout then uses its algorithms to compute your "True Reach," "Network," and "Amplification," and assign you a Klout score from 1 to 100. (Average Klout score is 20.) You also see your friend's scores, and you can give away +K icons to acknowledge that they have influenced you. Adding to the fun is the Klout Perks department where brands make swag gifts available to tastemakers they feel might boost their product via word of mouth. Getting offered a particular perk depends upon your Klout score, gender and age. This site has great graphics and is an engagement model worthy of study. The science behind condensing your entire online presence into one number may be oversimplified—but it's hard to resist.

Google Alerts (www.google.com/alerts)

Admittedly, Alerts seems like the answer to a "What doesn't fit in this group?" quiz. Alerts don't measure engagement or schedule posts, but they can find people that are engaging with you and your brand. People that are talking about you are likely to be good prospects for brand engagement. This information can be leveraged in interactive ways. A Twitter search can also pay dividends. For example, set up a Tweetdeck column that includes your brand name (not Twitter handle) and over time it will pay dividends.

Summary

Don't be afraid to jump in and try a few items from the social media digital toolbox. Like all other quadrants in the online space, developing (and understanding) metrics that can help you succeed is a building experience. If this chapter gets just one point across, I hope it will be to give you the confidence to start clicking on all these tools. That's the best way to learn and become more skilled.

But a second point to consider is the realization that content *quality* trumps *quantity*. So when you are deciding the best way to orchestrate your posting pathways across all the different platforms you use, do not let your quest for efficiency obscure the value of the work itself. Let your content dictate the best course. Your goal in all of this is not just efficiency, but to shine, sparkle and engage. Finding shortcuts is a bonus, but of little value without great content.

Finally, please focus on one more word—*consistency*. Use scheduling software and/or set aside certain times of the day in your routine, but try to post something every day. I have been unable to find any scientific evidence on this, (if you do please let me know), but my personal anecdotal evidence suggests that to grow your audience you must be consistent. Look across your networks and identify a few of the folks that are posting all the time. Then watch to see how their followers, circles, likes, etc. are growing. It works!

Chapter 10
Stay Out At Sea Long Enough To Learn About Being A Captain

"Is direct marketing, using email and social media, advertising or marketing?"

This question reminds me of the popular ad slogan which asked, "Is [Certs] a breath mint, or a candy mint?" The answer, provided in the commercial and clearly intended to influence your thinking was, "It's two: two mints in one."

This brilliant campaign promoted the idea that the innocent little sugar mint was suddenly worth twice its previous value because it served two purposes. So if asked "Is *The Secrets of the List* marketing or publicity?" The answer is, "It's two, two functions at the same time."

Marketing is generally thought to include paid advertising situations where a brand is placed in front of consumers. Publicity is the act of using an event to draw media attention to a brand. But today, social media has truly grayed the lines between these two sales disciplines.

Your website contains an ad for your product which seems to clearly be a marketing strategy. But there is also a story about how someone uses your product in a unique way. That's more like publicity. And what about people that read the story and engage by leaving a comment? Is that marketing or publicity? Probably some of each.

The digital universe rarely mirrors the physical world, so do not be surprised when situations arise requiring a unified, multi-prong strategy. Don't let yourself get hung up on the definitions, instead ask yourself, "What is needed to get results?"

The point here is that things are changing rapidly, and will continue to do so. As you proceed down the list-building pathway outlined in this book please remain alert to what is happening around you. Focus on the concepts, not the details. In addition, if you keep your eyes on the changing world of technology hardware, you'll be able to spot trends long before they gain mainstream recognition. For example, you were probably aware of the power of smartphones several years ago (if you already owned one), and realized they would gain a majority share in the mobile space. Smartphones are enablers of everything digital and social media. If you saw them becoming more popular, then it would be an easy jump to guess that social networks would also continue to grow in popularity. That knowledge would have placed you way ahead of mainstream media and might have given you the idea to jump into social media right away. So do some regular homework and try new things. (According to mobile research firm Comscore as of January 2012 there are over 100 million smartphone subscriptions in the U.S.)

Engagement is a word often used in these pages, but recently its definition is also attracting heated discussion. In the Feb. 27, 2012 issue of *Advertising Age*[17] Simon Dumenco writes, "Many social-media 'experts' insist that a 'two-way conversation' between marketers and consumers is the whole point of social and anything less than that is a reflection of outdated, broadcast-style thinking. But the reality is that many people follow and 'friend' brands simply because they want to hear from these brands, not necessarily talk back."

An Ehrenberg-Bass Institute report quoted in the article supports Dumenco's premise, "...slightly more than 1% of fans of the biggest brands on Facebook are actually engaging with the brands."

It's a fair question. Does every consumer desire to actively participate in the discussion, or are some content to passively sit back, listen and watch? Creating the possibility for a one-to-one relationship and two-way conversation

---

17 The Brutal Truth About Social Media: It's OK To Be A Little Antisocial, Simon Dumenco. Advertising Age, February 27, 2012.

between brand and consumer is perhaps the most often cited advantage of the online era. It's considered a massively powerful tool when compared with traditional media's broadcast-only ability. Dumenco, however, finds a middle ground between active and passive online engagement by drawing an interesting comparison between what print media calls pass-along readership and the retweet or posting of articles on various social networks.

"Retweeting is the thing followers of @adage and @okgo seem to do most," Dumenco notes. "It's a form of engagement, sure, but a retweet is at its core a republication. *Ad Age* and OK Go are essentially broadcasters of content and some of our 'fans' volunteer to serve basically as broadcast-repeating stations via social media."

At the beginning of this book I asked the question, "What if you could grow your company's bottom line, become more competitive, acquire new customers and enhance your ability to market more effectively… without breaking the bank?"

It's worth repeating again, because that is our goal. Do we care how our fans are relating to us? If they prefer broadcasted information or want to participate in a two-way conversation? If they desire active or passive engagement? NO. We want their attention. We want them to give us permission to communicate with them and we'd like to occupy a top-of-mind position in their brand universe, but how they choose to manage the relationship is not a key ingredient.

Understanding that each person's comfort zone and preferences will be different means looking beyond obvious performance metrics to discern what is really going on. Maybe you're not getting as many responses as think you should, but your list continues to get signups and your website traffic is growing. That may not be cause for alarm. The amount and types of response you receive will be contingent upon your specific brand. For example, people are more likely to comment about general subjects like recipes and music than they are on personal topics like sexuality. Trying different ideas is the only way you can determine the right mix. But above all, stay calm, be constant and focus on what fits with your brand. Don't abandon ship, stay out at sea long enough to learn about being a captain.

Be Content

It's gratifying to watch the mainstream discussion discover something that you have been aware of and benefitting from for a long while. In this case the idea of "Content Marketing." That term is directly connected to many of the chapters in this book. Content that appeals to your consumers can be a "carrot" that attracts them to you like a powerful magnet. It can lead them through the Digital Jungle to arrive on your website's doorstep and ultimately convince them to become part of your email mailing list.

"Corporations are pushing out news stories, infographics and documentary-style videos as if they were run by a

Frankenstein combo of Henrys Ford and Luce," says Matthew Creamer in the annual 2012 Digital Issue of *Advertising Age*.[18] "Forget press releases and ads. What matters is straightforward, practical, even non-promotional information that plays well on social networks."

Unfortunately, not all brands understand that good content is not purchased by the pound like bologna at a supermarket deli counter. It requires professional curation and creators.

"Quality comes from understanding that creating content isn't the same as PR, and it certainly isn't advertising," says Creamer. "Seems like an obvious point, but wade through the deepening thicket of content programs and you get mixed results. For every American Express *Open Forum* or Red Bull *Art of Flight*, there are many more crap ones, graveyards."

Content marketing, like many new ideas in the world of publicity and marketing started out being adopted by smaller companies looking to find a way to compete against larger corporations with larger budgets. Eventually, anecdotal success stories emerged. Finally, the professional marketing community is now trying to give the idea its formal blessing by quantifying the concept and measuring its ROI (return on investment) as compared with conventional strategies.

---

18 Content: Marketing's Best Hope Or More Hype? by Matthew Creamer. Advertising Age, February 27, 2012.

"PR agencies are coming to us and saying that the cost per impression of creating content and having people share it is much lower than buying StumbleUpon or clicks or ads," Creamer's article quotes Contently.com co-founder Shane Snow. Creamer also quotes Weber Shandwick Digital Content Manager, Parker Ward. "With an effective content engine, it costs less to bring a visitor to a platform through content than display advertising. User behavior of opt-in referrals from 'content' sources—[like] search, return visits, social channel promotion, syndication partners—encourages them to stay longer and be more engaged."

As outlined in Chapters 3 and 6, there are myriad ways to produce and display your content. Be flexible and stay within your means. If you can afford a room full of genius journalists, that's great. But if not, you can still successfully "win" with content marketing. Invite your readers to share something, a photo of a child, a dog or a new way they used your product. Bolster your site with widgets or opinion polls. Upload photos of your company employees in action, interacting with customers. Let your imagination run free. Even a picture of a cat playing with a ball of string can be "content" if it somehow fits with your brand. The sum of having an email list, social media and a branded website places enormous power at your fingertips, but you must be patient while learning to unleash its full potential.

Summary

You can do this! Especially if you remember that patience is your friend. You are not building something finite, like a house or a bridge. You have embarked upon a journey with no end. However, as you travel you will find numerous stopping points where you can take a moment to look back and see how far you've come. It's a smart idea to keep a spreadsheet of your progress. When did you start each social network page, your website, and other destinations? Write down monthly growth totals and basic metrics like the numbers of followers, friends and contacts you have acquired. Include how many page views per month are you averaging on your website and of course the size of your email list. These numbers will grow over time and help you realize the scale of what you are accomplishing.

I invite you to visit www.secretsofthelist.com and sign up for the mailing list or follow me on Twitter (@davidmross). I will follow you back if you indicate you have read the book. The links to my other "pages" can be found at the beginning of this book and of course on the "Secrets" website.

I'd love to hear about your experiences—good and bad—with this book. What is your site like? Are you having success with the content you are using? What kinds of problems are you facing? Which social networks seem to be the most important for your audience?

My intention is to update the material online and share your comments. Together we can learn from each other's experiences—the wrong turns and the successes. Email me at dross@bossross.com. And thanks so much for reading...

—David M. Ross

Appendix A
Lowenstein's Rules Of Engagement

When it comes to engaging your friends, followers and subscribers there is no one way to be successful. In fact, although there are some great lists and general rules to follow (see Chapters 4, 5), each company or individual must find their own voice. Ultimately, it means developing a unique way to translate general guidelines into something specific that fits smoothly with your personality and/or the character of your brand.

Musician Jaron Lowenstein aka Jaron And The Long Road To Love (JATLRTL), has found some innovative ways to leverage social media and consented to talk about them in an interview, specifically for this book (12/1/2011). His humorous single "Pray For You," which he co-wrote, went Top 20 on country radio (2010) and sold over one million downloads. Lowenstein was also half of Evan and Jaron, a duo with his identical twin, that had the multi-platinum selling song "Crazy For This Girl" in the late '90s. He is an active student of social media and fan engagement. On Facebook (12/10/11), JATLRTL has over

160,000 likes. His Twitter feed has over 9,000 followers and his YouTube channel, Jaronwoodvideo has close to 13 million views.

"Social media today is all about ME," says Lowenstein. "It should be called MeBook (not Facebook). No longer is access to the world limited by a handful of gatekeepers, everyone has the opportunity to reach the world with a click. But conversely, with billions of new channels, it's increasingly difficult to break through the clutter and be noticed."

Engage Means Interact

"Engage your audience doesn't mean talk *to* them. People are engaged when they're the center of attention. When I write a post or tweet about my audience or ask for their input, interaction consistently increases tenfold. For example, if I post 'Just got out of the studio, can't wait for you to hear this new song!' the interaction is light. But if I post 'You guys ever been in a recording studio? If yes, tell me about it. I'm wondering because I just got out of the studio and I never get tired of recording. I love it! Can't wait for you to hear this new song I might add!' then interaction explodes.

"I am able to communicate the same info, but by asking them to share something, it gives them a deeper level of involvement instead of just breezing by my comment. Sometimes we think that brevity is better when engaging and that's not always the case."

Lowenstein continues, "Let's say you have a website and are trying to get people's information. You'll ask for name, city, zip code and email address and you'll keep it short so as not to put out your fans or customers. But nobody fills those out. You know why? Because it's boring and information for you, not for them. But if you give them 10 questions to answer about them, they're much more likely to answer. You can ask the questions in a fun way and ascertain the same information you would get with the boring questions. For example, instead of asking 'Male or female?' ask 'Which movie do you like better *Any Given Sunday* or *Twilight?*' Or 'Food Network or ESPN?' Plus you can still keep some of the boring questions as long as you weave them in between fun ones.

"Conventional wisdom says everyone's on the go, and has no time, but people aren't nearly as busy as they pretend to be. They make time for the things they want to do. Conventional wisdom is partially right, just not fully updated. It's like some marketers are running software in their heads from twenty years ago. You have to be willing to update in real time if you are going to play this game because the world has changed more in the last twenty years than it has since the beginning of time. And it's set to do it again."

Update frequently

"If you can become a site that people know changes daily or multiple times each day, you can build a sustainable audience. It's less about your commitment to the readers and more about the fact that we're all a bunch of stimulation junkies who by 10 a.m. have already checked every website we frequent and have nothing else new to consume. It's what makes Facebook and Twitter so popular. The constant influx of new stories, ideas, information, etc.

"The world wide web is cluttered with billions of websites, yet the average person doesn't go to more than five in a given day. If you're visiting over 10 websites in a day you're in a very small majority. Think about it. I'm not talking about where you go when you link out, just the landing pages. What sites do you visit daily? Facebook, Twitter, Yahoo, Google, Amazon, Hulu, DrudgeReport and a porn site or two? Whatever it is, it's less than 10 for most of us. The common thread between all of these sites is they frequently update their content. When you realize how few sites we go to on a daily basis you realize how under-developed the web is and just how much more room there is for something remarkable."

Being a good student of human behavior, Lowenstein advises, begins with knowing oneself. "There are plenty of clever ways to get people to engage," he notes. "But first you have to engage with yourself. Before I came back to music I was writing comedy for years. My writing partner was the hugely talented Whitney Cummings from the show *Whitney,* now on NBC. What I learned about comedy is that the truth is funny. To connect with people we must be honest, be willing to make fun of ourselves and really observe. When you can talk about the ugly underneath, your fears and the things that annoy you, people also laugh because they go, 'Ooh that's me, you're speaking for me.' Through writing comedy I learned we are all so similar. Our similarities are how I know that 10 fun questions will work on your site. I know that I will stop what I'm doing to take a silly IQ test that shows me a picture of some schmuck and asks me if I think I'm smarter than he is. They can sell me two hours of ads while I'm taking this stupid test just to prove my manhood. The irony is, I've already proven I'm an idiot just by taking the IQ test.

"Remember the website 'Am I Hot Or Not?' It exploded because people got to share their opinions. It was a wretched site, but people sat for hours, clicking through thousands of pictures of women and rating them. So pay attention to your habits, good or bad, and engage with that knowledge. The secret to getting lists and engaging people is to write something that you yourself would click on."

To test Lowenstein's advice I created my own fun questions poll on www.SecretsofTheList.com. The site was still very new (12/8/11) and so the experiment was on a small scale. Using a Wordpress plugin (WP-Polls), I created a seven question survey and tried to make them humorous, but also about meaningful subjects including the upcoming Presidential election, global warming, cable TV bills, mobile phones, music and marriage. Over a three-day period the number of poll voters was 170% higher than the number of people who signed up for our prominently displayed newsletter which asked only for email and first name. Not a scientific survey, but it made me realize that placing the newsletter signup at the bottom of the poll would probably improve our visitor conversion and increase the size of our list more rapidly. It certainly whetted my appetite to experiment more with this approach.

Unblending

During our interview, Lowenstein discussed another engagement technique, something he refers to as "Unblending,"—making a conscious attempt to deliberately stand out.

"Most people are asleep at the wheel going through their days on cruise control," says Lowenstein. "Your mind will run itself. Grocery stores and other retailers spend millions to make things easy and intuitive for you. They don't want to wake you up. So to get someone's attention you have to unblend. Have you ever looked at a site and seen a typo, a misused word or an extra space? Somehow it bothers you and wakes you up a bit. When I make mistakes it gets attention and my feedback goes up 100x. People want me to know they are smarter than me, but in the process of correcting the mistake they are talking about what I'm selling. They're in the game and activity goes up. When I create Facebook ads I sometimes spell things wrong—not cool wrong, just wrong. Social media gives you the key to reach tens of thousands of people or more, but it falls on deaf ears unless it's a.) Something they care about, b.) Breaking news, or c.) Someone needing their opinion. Anything else and my conversion rate is pathetic.

"It has to be *remarkable*, if you want people to remark about it," he continues. "Often it's because it's extreme. The dumbest thing you've ever seen, or the funniest, or the nicest. Or perhaps it's a genuine emotional moment that people feel compelled to talk about because they know their friends will. I'm a big Steve Jobs fan. He said, 'It's not enough to be really good. If it's not sensational no one cares.' And that's how it is with social media. If it's not *incredible* it just dies in the crowd. All the money in the world can't artificially push something through the web. But if it's really incredible, exceptional, polarizing it will take off on its own."

Summary

Learning to engage your audience is perhaps as much art as it is craft. And like so many things in life, the devil is in the details. For example, Lowenstein's "Unblending" concept can be applied in myriad creative ways. But care must be taken that your approach fits your brand and enhances it's image. If your brand is an English language school for example, then deliberately making grammatical mistakes in your ads (as Lowenstein mentions can work with his music fans), might cast doubt on the quality of the school and not be the right tactic. One must be willing to experiment using a variety of ideas with the purpose of creating a tailor-made strategy to fit your specific situation.

Some of the best techniques are the simplest. For example, as mentioned above, successful sites are updated frequently. Why then, would you operate a site that isn't updated daily? Or perhaps the better question to ask is, "What kinds of content can my site feature that is within our means to update daily?" If you are working by yourself it may be unrealistic to assume that you will be able to crank out a handful of new articles every day while running your business at the same time. Conversely, if hiring a room full of journalists and in effect becoming a hybrid publication built around supporting a brand is within your means, it's a powerful strategy.

Lowenstein's comment, "Social media gives you the key to reach tens of thousands of people or more, but it falls on deaf ears unless it's a.) Something they care about, b.) Breaking news, or c.) Someone needing their opinion," deserves repeating. Breaking news can be a great way to "update frequently" with something people value. It proved the perfect strategy for *MusicRow* in 2008 when we began tweeting headlines 'n' links. At that time it was a new tactic and our Twitter list started growing rapidly. Today, most every publication uses this technique and brands are becoming increasingly involved in producing, creating and distributing content.

Julie Liesse writes about *Top Trends For 2012*[19] in the November 28, 2011 *Advertising Age*. She is featured in a special section hosted by the Council of Public Relations

---

19 Top Trends For 2012, by Julie Liesse, Advertising Age, Nov. 28, 2011

Firms. Liesse writes, "The focus in 2012 will be on engagement—not merely 'likes,' or fans or followers. Liesse quotes Bret Werner, managing partner of PR firm Catalyst who says, "There are a lot of brands with heavy fan bases, but low engagement—consumers who click to 'like' something, but never go back to their social network page. The real question is: How do I further engage my consumers?"

Liesse also states, "Social media will rely increasingly on professionally produced content..." She quotes Jonathan Kopp, global director for Ketchum Digital who says, "To the internet user it is all content. People are starting to lose the distinction between whether they are reading the *New York Times* or what a friend has passed on."

Looked at another way, Kopp's observation means that sites aggregating/filtering content can be just as valuable to users as the entities that create and produce it. This trend creates great opportunities for brands who want to have a frequently updated site, but don't have the resources to do all the heavy lifting. Now it is possible to find a unique way to aggregate headlines or RSS feeds and engage at the same time.

Social media and engaging followers is a fluid space. Be prepared to experiment, try new things, imitate and rethink strategies. One pillar of success, however will likely remain constant. Know your customers, encourage their feedback and listen to what they tell you. Using social media, the one-on-one communication between you and your followers can be more detailed than ever before in the history of business marketing. But with the increasingly open pathways comes greater responsibility and higher expectations for all partners in the process.

Appendix B
Here In The Real World

Traveling from the halls of academia to the board-rooms, where theory and practice create commerce, provides an essential perspective. And measuring the elasticity required in moving from the hypothetical, to real world truths, is a journey that takes experience and time to assess. This appendix features comments and insights from a selection of entrepreneurs who are uniquely integrating social media and email marketing concepts into their business and personal routines.

Jennie Smythe of Nashville-based Girlilla Marketing, a boutique online marketing company that works with artists such as Zac Brown Band, Sugarland and Colt Ford, nicely summed how crowded the fight for consumer attention is becoming at the start of the 2011 holiday season. She never uses the word "trust," but you can read it between the lines. She's focused on the music industry, but her comments are equally important for all brands.

"If you've spent any time looking at the ads or displays targeted at consumers this holiday season," Smythe writes, "it's not hard to understand why the fan is much more likely to be *in* the clouds instead of being excited to *use* a cloud-based service. Your artist is on Facebook, Twitter, Google+, has an email list, a QR code, a store with a promo code, exclusive content at so-and-so.com, plus ten different album packages with different tracks at different retailers. They are also offering a pre-order opportunity using the latest technology, streaming on Spotify and the list goes on. But, where's the music? Where's the connection? What really matters? What cuts through the clutter is word of mouth by a trusted source and there's no formula for that. If the technology is your marketing angle and you are just crossing things off your to-do list, you are going to fail. Lead with the music. Be calm, patient and respectful of your fans and ALL of the things they need to buy, not just music."

Tony Conway, who currently steers Conway Entertainment Group's three divisions, has always been an early adopter, stretching all the way back to the fax machine. "I believe we had the first fax machine in Nashville," Conway reminisced. "We did a deal with IBM for Farm Aid in 1985 and installed faxes from the front of the stage out to the mixing board because there were 60 some acts involved and it was a great way to stay in touch." Conway's enviable career has placed him in charge of live events and artists acting as a talent agent, promoter and manager. During his 25-year career in country music he's worked with a who's who of artist royalty such as Garth Brooks, George Strait, Jason Aldean and Bill Monroe, and he's also represented pop artists such as Joe Cocker, Alice Cooper, Blood Sweat And Tears and the Beach Boys.

Conway's present day social media strategy aligns his social networking accounts by divisions. "We do different things with different groups of people in each company," he explains. Therefore he has three Twitter accounts and a similar setup for Facebook. "We use social media in everything we do and have a staff person that specializes in that function," he says. "In the management world I'm dealing with other managers, attorneys, publicists, business managers, artists, road managers, band members, bus, sound and light companies. I'm not trying to market the management company, so we don't publicize it much, but using social media to exchange information with those specific parties works well. Our Talent Agency division is different. It markets to over 12,000 talent buyers worldwide. But whenever possible I narrow our talent marketing to the group or groups most likely to fit the message. That generally results in a higher email open rate."

Unlike many of the B2C (business to consumer) examples in this book, Conway's marketing efforts are mostly B2B (business to business). Because he is dealing directly with other businesses as clients it means that his email lists do not have to be grown organically, they can be acquired. "It's something you learn from being in the profession," Conway notes. "You collect it, absorb it and buy it. There are several publications we buy lists from that take the time and patience to get the information correct." Conway's main thrust is via email marketing, but he also engages with these contacts on social media including You-Tube. "YouTube has replaced showcasing for us," he says. "There's nothing comparable to a live concert, but it has helped immensely. Before YouTube I used to say, 'I'll send you a DVD,' or 'The artist will be on *Leno* tomorrow.' It was hit and miss. But now while we are talking on the phone I can direct them to our channel or email them a link and watch it together."

Conway utilizes some interesting strategies to reach consumers. "We use social networks to help market shows and sell tickets for our CEG Live division, with contests, pre-sales and by interacting with artist fan clubs," he says. "Often we have 30-40 artists on a festival and each one has a fan club and their own followers. Usually 1-2 weeks before tickets go on sale to the general public the artist will tell their fans they can buy special pre-sale VIP tickets to the event. We sell a lot of tickets that way. For example, if a fan is enamored with Dierks Bentley and follows him on the road, they may already be at their computer waiting to find out when he is going to play Atlanta. I couldn't buy that kind of advertising on radio, TV or newspaper. So we market first through social media and then traditional media. But now when I buy radio I also buy banners on the station websites and they tweet to their listeners about exclusive contests we do with each station for backstage winners and signed guitars. Our ticket companies will aggressively market, too. It's amazing what Ticketmaster can do to help sales. Fans can even see where their Facebook friends will be sitting for the show. And there are other ticket companies like Ticketfly and Elevate that specialize in social media marketing.

"Say you are doing a New Orleans blues concert. Many ticketing companies have a database that includes everyone that ever bought a ticket to a blues concert in the surrounding states. They will send those fans texts and an email blast about your show. It is direct marketing at its finest."

Ticketing companies have a strong "carrot" which helps them acquire email addresses from fans anxious to purchase tickets. The addresses become part of a massive database which also includes the preferences of each individual based upon the shows they attended. Once the emails are matched with social network accounts, the database comes alive.

Another viral strategy Conway employs to build excitement for an upcoming event is the in-home artist concert. "An in-home concert is a contest where a fan gets picked to have a live concert in their house and invite up to 50 people to attend," says Conway. "You can also do a webcast so it goes all over the world. You get a huge audience watching and they talk about it for months. For the fan that won the concert—and the friends they invited—it's a big deal. Of course we collect email addresses from everyone involved."

• •

The term record promotion used to describe the process of trying to secure airplay for artists on the radio. Today that vision has expanded into a broader career outlook. Nine North's Larry Pareigis and Kevin Mason are fast becoming the poster image for a promotion company adopting new media as a vital part of its tool set. Nashville-based, the company is extremely active on a variety of social networks. Pareigis has over 50,000 Twitter followers (@ninenorthLP; 1/2/12) and casts a long shadow over additional nets such as Google+, Get Glue, MySpace, Tumblr, LinkedIn and of course Facebook. Director of Top Secret Projects, Kevin Mason who also runs Intensity Media, has been active in helping raise Pareigis and Nine North's profile, plus using the companies growing online influence to help the artists they promote.

"The world we live in is no longer about business entities, it is about people with entities," says Mason. "And this is part of our strategy. Nine North has a lot of its own pages and Larry has separate pages too. Larry is the star of Nine North in building the brand. So by mixing it all together, with both the company and Larry's profiles, we're able to put a human face on a company brand. That's what the future of marketing is all about. Everyone is worried about privacy. You wouldn't know it from seeing him on social media, but Larry is one of the most private people I know. Online you only see what he allows you to see. And that's the key to this, understanding how to present yourself and not just throwing everything out there. Mostly we promote Nine North as a brand to the music community—artists, managers, etc. Not to the fans. By putting Larry's individual face on the company when consumers get into what he is doing they also get acquainted with our artists. Email marketing is the next step in that process. We think about creating the master list every day. It's our next evolutionary step. We've created these little armies at Twitter and Facebook. We don't pester them with requests for data, but when you need help, and set it up as a one click thing, they go to work for you. They become a force."

"Building that fan base one address at a time is invaluable," agrees Pareigis. "One thing beautifully unique about the country music format is if you are talented and engage with a fan base, they will be stuck on you for life. So not only are we working on traditional airplay for our artist clients, but at the same time we assist them in their efforts to build fans 24/7/365."

"What's the next big thing," asks Pareigis rhetorically. "There isn't one." He believes that artists and brands need to be in lots of places, not just the next big thing. The trick is to find the right mix to fit each situation. "Every artist needs a custom suit," says Pareigis. "One that will fit them perfectly. It's our job to help create and tailor that suit. We are being engaged for our expertise as tailors in those areas."

Appendix C
Could New Data Blueprints Redefine Our World?

Can you imagine a world without data? Probably not. Surrounding us everywhere is a constantly changing information matrix that flows like an infinite stream. We process this data in many ways, the most common of which is through our five senses—touch, smell, sight, taste and sound. You hear the sound of a siren while driving on the interstate, smell fresh cookies baking in the oven, feel another's soft skin, taste your favorite dessert or enjoy seeing a beautiful sunset over the ocean. Sensory data can also trigger powerful remembrances of people, events or time periods.

But what if the world of data is larger and more complex than we imagine it to be? For example, could an intricate ceiling shadow produced by an outside light shining through the vertical blinds on a corner window be more than just a static image? The shadow changes whenever the characteristics of the objects projecting it are changed, therefore it seems logical to assume the shadow is a kind of data-blueprint expressing the relationship of these objects, and if/when translated properly, would allow them to be exactly reproduced. We could expand the concept of the data stream even further. Take songs for example. Yes, we listen to music using one of our five senses, but can that really be all that is taking place as we process musical data? If it was just sound, then why do some songs make us smile, cry or laugh while others do not? Perhaps we are reacting to other data streams embedded in the musical experience that we are not aware of, but somehow affect our emotions nonetheless. Art in general seems to have "hidden" yet unpredictable data attached to it, streams capable of producing strong reactions. The stronger the message and the more people that "get" the message and feel an emotion, then the more highly praised is the artist and the work.

In addition to data from our five senses and more intangible sources like the vaguely defined receptors we call emotions, there are other data flows which have cause and effect relationships in our world. Of massive consequence for example, is the written word and other symbols, such as the science of mathematics. The importance of these data flows in fact separates man from all other creatures.

Alfred Korzybski, author of *Science and Sanity* wrote a short essay titled "What I Believe," in 1948 as a contribution to a symposium where he was trying to offer a condensed version and summary of his work. The essay is included in his second edition of his first book, *Manhood of Humanity*. "Humans," he writes, "... are uniquely characterized by the capacity of an individual or a generation to begin where the former left off. I called this essential capacity 'time-binding.' This can be accomplished only by a class of life which uses symbols as means for time-binding. Such a capacity depends on and necessitates 'intelligence', means of communication, etc. On this inherently human level of interdependence time-binding leads inevitably to feelings of responsibility, duty toward others and the future, and therefore to some type of ethics, morals, and similar social and/or socio-cultural reactions."

Korzybski's fascination with time-binding extended into a brilliant treatise dealing with the social development of mankind. But it also has additional concepts that directly apply to our discussion of data and how it is generally interpreted. He writes…

"Linguistic and grammatical structures also have prevented our understanding of human reactions. For instance, we used and still use a terminology of 'objective' and 'subjective', both extremely confusing, as the so-called 'objective' must be considered a construct made by our nervous system and what we call 'subjective' may also be considered 'objective' for the same reasons.

"My analysis showed that happenings in the world outside our skins, and also such organismal psychological reactions inside our skins as those we label 'feelings', 'thinking', 'emotions', 'love', 'hate', 'happiness', 'unhappiness', 'anger', 'fear', 'resentment', 'pain', 'pleasure', etc. occur only on the non-verbal, or what I call silent levels. Our speaking occurs on the verbal levels, and we can speak about, but not on, the silent or un-speakable levels."

Mathematics is very capable of capturing details in the objective world, but as yet it lacks the ability to describe the subjective world.

What Korzybski points out in these passages is that when we try to talk about 'subjective' human reactions or emotions that live on 'un-speakable' levels using 'objective' means such as language, then the best we can do is to find words that 'represent' these emotions, but words can never be the same as the 'reality' behind them. When applied to the empirical study of data these concepts open the door, through deductive reasoning, to the idea that there could be additional info streams of which we are presently un-aware.

High frequency sound provides an example of this distinction. A special dog whistle creates a sound which cannot be heard by human ears, and yet canines hear the sound and respond to it. What if there were other such data streams that cannot be received using our human senses or emotions? Perhaps there are streams that cannot be represented with symbols, because like subjective human reactions, they too live on levels that remain unspeakable due to a lack of the symbols necessary to properly describe them. If we are unable to experience or process this data it would therefore be impossible to know if it contains solutions to long term problems that seem unsolvable. For example, if potholes in the sidewalk were invisible to the human eye, one would wonder why they occasionally fell while walking to the store. Without being able to see the hole in the sidewalk, falling would appear to be a random experience when in reality it might be explained and more importantly prevented if one could process the data properly and 'see' the potholes.

In our culture we have reports of individuals who were able to talk with people that had died, heal, do magic, or find a missing person. Without the science to confirm or explain these happenings our culture tends to either attribute them to happenstance or place them on a spiritual pedestal. But what if these individuals possessed special abilities that allowed them to receive a data stream that few others were able to process? It would certainly explain this type of behavior. In fact, it seems perfectly reasonable to assume that there *are* additional data streams of which we are unaware.

But unfortunately, invisible or undetected data cannot (has not) been folded into time-binding and therefore any lesson or societal benefit that might have been derived from the stream of a 'special abilities' individual is foregone. Are there data streams that might hold keys to scientific problems which we have as yet been unable to solve? Perhaps. Could cures for some of our worst diseases be right in front of us, if we could only receive their message? Perhaps.

One way to dig deeper into this area would be to enrich the expressive capabilities of our written symbols. Mathematics is very capable of capturing details in the objective world, but as yet it lacks the ability to describe the subjective world.

Surely there must be data streams that can only be translated or received with senses we don't possess or haven't yet developed. The first step to understanding these new data flows may be as basic as simply admitting the possibility of their existence. Ultimately the quest to explore more fully the world around us may open up science and art to goals as yet undreamed.

At The Crossroads Again—This Time The Music Industry Should Innovate And Legislate

The New Year toasts are over and 2012 stretches before us like the red and blue lines on an analog road map. Life's complexities, and the challenges facing the music industry, make planning for the future a good bit more difficult than simply taking a drive from Nashville to Atlanta. Offering support is a new signpost on the music model highway—"Access," the ability to listen where and when you want. And it's beginning to gain critical mass.

Survival, in business and one's personal life is more like a chess game than a map-reading experience because it is multi-dimensional—results and opportunities are continually readjusting in real time. In navigating life's journey, it helps immensely to have a realization about the goals most important to your passage. Business is also subject to discovering people's wants and needs. Locating these compass points makes one more likely to create and implement solutions with beneficial effects.

The music industry has been operating without a compass for more than a decade. Instead of electing to investigate and formulate strategy which might equitably rebalance the digital relationship between music creators and consumers the industry has remained stuck on a treadmill, ineffectually reacting as the machine slows and gains speed. The results have been catastrophic.

Album sales in the U.S. have plummeted -58% since 2000 and we have seen the size and power of the record labels diminish accordingly. Fourteen years ago there were six major labels offering creative diversity and stimulating competition. As we peer into 2012 we see the imminent demise of once proud EMI, a great label which introduced many amazing talents to the world's pop culture—leaving us with three major labels.

The digital era arrived loaded with promise and new opportunities. It should have been a ladder to greater heights, not a chute to diminished expectations. Is it too late? Can anything still be done to rebuild a more supportive climate for creators, artists and rights holders? The answer is "Yes."

At the turn of the century, copyright owners were busy trying to solve their digital concerns in the courtroom. And at first it looked like they might succeed. Napster, the first peer-to-peer file network to popularize music sharing, had accumulated over 60 million active users. It was a marketer's dream, but labels chose to litigate it out of business instead of benefit from its power. Why? Most obvious was that a giant community had gathered that was sharing music for free. But labels could have negotiated with Napster and found a way to monetize it. I believe what really irked the labels most was the issue of distribution. Labels had always controlled the musical distribution channels and therefore its supply, demand and pricing. Because they were not well informed, labels believed they could regain control using a digital lock that came to be known as DRM or digital rights management. They were wrong. Twelve years later, the tactics of litigation and DRM proved a severe miscalculation. Napster was shuttered, but new more difficult-to-track P2P technologies replaced it.

A Do Over?

Today the music industry is quite possibly at the crossroads of another great opportunity we call "Access." Music technologies like Spotify, Google Music, iCloud, Rdio, MOG, Pandora and others are connecting consumers to almost all recorded music. Each system offers a slightly different arrangement of services, most of which are subscriber and ad-based. Consumers are clearly enjoying this freedom of choice and the ability to listen whenever and wherever they choose and both free and paid subscribers are starting to grow.

What is making this possible? The deep deployment of broadband internet and high speed mobile networks have greatly expanded the digital horizon. Music files that a few years ago were too large to stream comfortably at available speeds, today are easily boomeranged about like crickets in a cornfield. We also have rich communication networks (social networks) where word of mouth spreads at warp speed.

Consumers are liking these new ways to enjoy all the music, all the time at affordable costs. But can "Access" be developed to produce more revenue? Royalties from these streaming services are still meager. The streaming business needs to be allowed to benefit from economies of scale. Secondly, we have to find ways to help them attract larger numbers of users and thus set the scale/revenue effect in motion.

For example, Pandora and other streaming services are starting to attract users and advertisers, but unlike terrestrial radio, they must pay a set fee for every user/stream broadcast. If left unchanged, this stranglehold on profits will choke these services and then send consumers where? Yes, that's right, back to FREE.

Copyright owners need to be compensated for their intellectual property, but they need to be smart and think long term. That requires discussion about how these new services can best achieve scale and grow.

A low monthly copyright fee, collected by ISPs could be the best way to achieve this goal. The money would flow directly into a rights pool and then be distributed according to copyright use. Granted, a mandatory fee is like a tax and may not be embraced by everyone, but it is the best way to rapidly achieve scale. Unlike the brick and mortar world, consumers would pay on the way into the store. Once online they'd have unlimited choice and access to copyrighted materials. It would feel like Free, but be paid in advance.

The "Access" model is still new enough to make changes possible. However, this window will not stay open long. In some ways, it's like 2000 all over again except we now have the opportunity for a "do over." Perhaps this time we'll innovate and legislate. We're at the crossroads, again. Will we take advantage?

ABOUT THE AUTHOR

Born and raised in Boston, MA., David M. Ross graduated from the University of Pennsylvania Wharton School with a B.S. in Economics and later attended the Berklee College of Music, majoring in arranging.

After spending ten years on the road as a professional musician, Ross traveled to Nashville and in April 1981 founded *MusicRow* magazine which he sold in 2008 after a successful 30-year reign as Publisher/CEO. During his time at *MusicRow* he profitably transformed the publication from print to digital by pioneering many of the email/social media marketing techniques revealed in *Secrets Of The List,* his first book-length writing project.

One of country music's most-read industry analysts, Ross continues to cover the intersection between Nashville's entertainment business and technology and speaks frequently at seminars, conferences and on panels.

He currently serves on the Board of Directors of The Country Music Hall of Fame and Museum and the Country Music Association. He received the CMA President's Award for Outstanding Service in 1998 and the Canadian Country Music Association's prestigious Leonard T. Rambeau Award for International Achievement in 2003.

David and wife Susana have been married for 37 years and have two children, Michelle and Isabel.

Unleash the Power of Social Media to leverage
your brand more effectively.

Learn the Rules of the Digital Jungle, why the
carrot is mightier than the stick and
how to create a Coordinated Strategy.

Your Friends, Followers and Likes
play an important role,
but if they don't lead to
"The List" and a
two-way conversation,
your plan is missing a key ingredient.

Don't let your quest for efficiency
obscure the value of the work itself.
Your goal is not just efficiency,
but to shine, sparkle and engage.

18924512R00070

Made in the USA
Lexington, KY
29 November 2012